D0875657

THE CULTURAL MIGRATION

This is a volume in the Arno Press collection

THE ACADEMIC PROFESSION

Advisory Editor
Walter P. Metzger

Editorial Board
Dietrich Goldschmidt
A. H. Halsey
Martin Trow

See last pages of this volume
for a complete list of titles.

The Cultural Migration
The European Scholar in America

by

Franz L. *Neumann, Henri Peyre, Erwin Panofsky*
Wolfgang Köhler, and Paul Tillich

Introduction by W. Rex Crawford

ARNO PRESS

A New York Times Company

New York / 1977

Editorial Supervision: MARIE STARECK

———◆———

Reprint Edition 1977 by Arno Press Inc.

Copyright 1953 by the University of
Pennsylvania Press

Reprinted by permission of the
University of Pennsylvania Press

THE ACADEMIC PROFESSION
ISBN for complete set: 0-405-10000-0
See last pages of this volume for titles.

Manufactured in the United States of America

———◆———

Library of Congress Cataloging in Publication Data

Main entry under title:

The Cultural migration.

  (The Academic profession)
  Reprint of the ed. published by the University
of Pennsylvania Press, Phildelphia, in series:
The Benjamin Franklin lectures of the University
of Pennsylvania, 5th ser., 1952.
  CONTENTS: Neumann, F.L. The social sciences.--
Peyre, H. The study of literature.--Panofsky, E.
The history of art. [etc.]
  1. United States--Intellectual life--20th
century--Addresses, essays, lectures. 2. Europe--
Intellectual life--Addresses, essays, lectures.
I. Neumann, Franz Leopold, 1900-   II. Series.
III. Series: Pennsylvania. University. Benjamin
Franklin lectures ; 1952.
[E169.1.C84 1977]   973.9   76-55140
ISBN 0-405-10041-8

THE BENJAMIN FRANKLIN LECTURES

OF THE

UNIVERSITY OF PENNSYLVANIA

FIFTH SERIES

THE BENJAMIN FRANKLIN LECTURES

CHANGING PATTERNS IN AMERICAN CIVILIZATION

by DIXON WECTER, F. O. MATTHIESSEN, DETLEV W. BRONK, BRAND BLANSHARD, and GEORGE F. THOMAS

Preface by ROBERT E. SPILLER

THE FUTURE OF DEMOCRATIC CAPITALISM

by THURMAN W. ARNOLD, MORRIS L. ERNST, ADOLF A. BERLE, JR., LLOYD K. GARRISON, and SIR ALFRED ZIMMERN

Introduction by S. HOWARD PATTERSON

THE ARTS IN RENEWAL

by LEWIS MUMFORD, PETER VIERECK, WILLIAM SCHUMAN, JAMES A. MICHENER, and MARC CONNELLY

Introduction by SCULLEY BRADLEY

THE SCIENTISTS LOOK AT OUR WORLD

by W. V. HOUSTON, W. ALBERT NOYES, JR., CURT STERN, ALAN GREGG, and WENDELL H. CAMP

Introduction by JOHN M. FOGG, JR.

THE CULTURAL MIGRATION

by FRANZ L. NEUMANN, HENRI PEYRE, ERWIN PANOFSKY, WOLFGANG KÖHLER, and PAUL TILLICH

Introduction by W. REX CRAWFORD

THE CULTURAL MIGRATION

The Cultural Migration
The European Scholar in America

by

Franz L. Neumann, Henri Peyre, Erwin Panofsky
Wolfgang Köhler, and Paul Tillich

Introduction by W. Rex Crawford

Philadelphia
UNIVERSITY OF PENNSYLVANIA PRESS
1953

Contents

Introduction

In spite of all the attention that has been given to the making of America by mass migration from Europe, one important aspect of the movement has received scant attention. The uprooted and transplanted intellectual deserves our study quite as much as the Polish peasant in America. Our social sciences, however, have been inclined to think in terms of millions rather than of individuals, and the humanities—in spite of meritorious work by Oscar Cargill and Edmund Wilson and, in older days, James Gibbons Huneker and Amy Lowell—have not chosen to put our relations to Europe in contemporary and personal terms.

It is just this accent on individual experience in our time which was in our minds in setting up the Benjamin Franklin Lectures for the spring of 1952. By asking each of the five distinguished lecturers to comment on his own experience, and to some extent on that of others in his own field, frankly expressing his criticisms of the methods used and the results achieved by American scholars in his discipline, and the gains to American scholarship resultant from the intellectual migration of the thirties, as well as his happy surprises in the American academic milieu, we hoped to elicit concrete contributions that would throw light on this limited but important area of acculturation. The result, which we now hope to share with a larger audience, fully justified our hopes. It obviously supports neither the 100 per cent American who feels that in all respects we are so far in advance of the rest of the world that we have nothing to learn, nor the unsympathetic opinion—so often encoun-

· 1

tered, for instance, in Latin America—that the only hope for culture in the United States is the transfer of some scores of Europeans to our shores in recent years. Rather it shows how we have been changed by our friends from European universities and how they themselves have changed in the process. Gains there have been on both sides, and Americans, as Professor Tillich brings out, have not been the only ones to lose provincialism. America has gained not only from the publication of scholarly books and the training given in seminars and laboratories, but it stands to gain from the thoughtful and insightful criticism so ironically and tolerantly phrased by our authors, and by their interpretation of the American reality to the rest of the world, which will doubtless pay more attention to their judgment than to what we say about ourselves.

That the list of European scholars who in recent years have enriched our academic life might have been vastly extended is of course apparent. One omission that I regret especially is that of a representative of the musicians who have come to do creative work in America, or if consistency requires remaining within the field of scholarship, of musicologists and historians of music. Such an addition might have revealed further variations of the kind that the reader will find for himself as he passes from social science to natural science and psychology, literature, art history, and religious thought in the pages that follow.

A special note of gratitude to Professor Franz Neumann is in order for having given us, in addition to reflection on his personal experience, an historical framework for all of the discussions, distinguishing the situation of the twentieth-century exile or refugee from that of earlier centuries, and subtly calling our attention to the possibility of a kind of inner or spiritual exile, an idea as provocative as Mr. Toynbee's colonization without colonists.

The invitation to *lege feliciter* can with honesty be accompanied by the grateful recording of the fact that it was most happily that Philadelphia audiences heard in their original form the chapters that are now offered to you.

W. R. C.

The Social Sciences

Franz L. Neumann

"If my country can do without me, I can do without her.
The world is large enough." Thus wrote Hugo Grotius,
the great "natural" and international lawyer after he had
succeeded, in 1621, in escaping imprisonment by Maurice
of Orange. For ten years he had to live in Paris, and it was
there, in exile, that he wrote his most famous book, *De jure
belli ac pacis.*

Yet the sentiment expressed by Grotius and his personal
fate must not lead us to believe that this is and can be
either the sentiment or the fate of the modern exile. Two
facts have changed radically: the role of the intellectual
and the social environment within which he lives.

The intellectual is, or ought to be, the critical conscience
of society in each of its historical periods. His role is to
deal critically with society, to show how far a society does
or rather does not realize freedom. Why this has to be so,
I cannot demonstrate here. It follows from the central conception of social and political theory: the conception of
freedom. This should be preserved by the intelligentsia.
But no society, past or present, being able to realize fully
man's freedom, the critical role of the intellectual in each
and every society necessarily follows. He is the conscience
of society. In a certain sense, therefore, he is always ostracized, for conscience is always inconvenient, particularly
in politics. Thus Socrates, in whom the critical role of the
intellectual is most impressively represented, refers to the

4 ·

philosopher as a "perennial metic," a permanent alien, who questions every form of government, every society as to its "philosophic nature."[1] This is Socrates' belief: "For I am and always have been one of those natures who must be guided by reason, whatever the reason may be which upon reflection appears to me the best; and now that this fate has befallen me, I cannot repudiate my own words."[2]

These meager generalizations of the intellectual's role may suffice here. They merely serve to prepare the analysis of the different fates suffered by the intellectual in different political systems.

Clearly, in the Greek city states, the role of the intellectual is the most difficult and the most endangered. Politics and culture are one or, at least, are presented as one. The civilization of the known world is concentrated in one spot so that the remaining world is, or appears to be, barbarian. Already, in view of the identity of culture and politics, exile means death.

In the Hellenistic-imperial period, however, the situation changes. A certain latitude is permitted to the intellectual, for he is tolerated if he is not political. Politics and culture are no longer identical. The Epicurean political philosophy aims precisely at legitimizing the political withdrawal of the intellectual who no longer expects from the state justice but mere maintenance of order and security, while Stoicism with its demands upon political morality leads to severe conflicts. Exile in this situation, although less damaging morally, is equally catastrophic intellectually. The lamentation of Ovid about his expulsion by Augustus to the shore of the Black Sea is a dramatic illustration of the frustrations of a poet so deeply part and

---

1 Plato, *Republic* (Cornford transl.) Bk. VI (Cornford Ch. XXII).
2 Plato, *Crito* (Jowett transl.). I have substituted for "chance" in the Jowett translation, the word "fate," which to the English reader seems to express the meaning better.

parcel of Roman civilization which he had done so much to raise to new levels.

The third situation is that of a universal culture, Christian in content, Latin in form and language, where exile often meant little more than a change of residence, where courts and universities often competed for exiled scholars, where national differences meant nothing; and widespread religious indifference, consequence of the dominant and unchallenged role of the Church in the cultural field, left to the exiled intellectual, no matter where, a fruitful field of activity. Indeed, the itinerant scholar—itinerant by choice or compulsion—is a quite normal phenomenon.

Yet there are exceptions. Here are two situations for which this general statement is not fully valid: namely, for the political scholar, and for heretics. I shall not deal with heresy here. Dante and Marsilius of Padua are symbols of the first. "How salty tastes the bread abroad and how difficult to mount and descend foreign staircases"— these words express Dante's feelings when he had to leave Florence. Yet he was a politician, poet, and scholar, and while exile destroyed, so to speak, the *homo politicus,* it brought to perfection the poet and scholar. Exile, in Dante's case, even changed, and changed fundamentally, his political conceptions. Verona, Bologna, Paris, Oxford, London, Cologne—to name but a few stations of his travels —led to his emancipation from narrow political provincialism to a political conception which, although without much influence in the fourteenth century, was to remain a challenge to provincialism and nationalism.

Another political scholar, Marsilius of Padua, exiled from Paris, simply entered the services of another political system—that of Louis of Bavaria—and through him attempted to put into practice his grandiose scheme of a wholly secular state which he had theoretically developed in his *Defensor Pacis.*

Yet it is important to realize—and important particularly for the full understanding of nationalism—that the period of the expansion of Christianity leads us back to the very first type: the total identification of culture and politics. A linguistic development will make clear what I mean.

Rome, as Greece earlier, often condemned the oppositional intellectual or artist to exile. The general term for this punishment is *exterminatio,* literally meaning expulsion beyond the frontiers. But the meaning of the term changed from about the third century A.D. and then assumed the meaning it now has—that of physical destruction.[3] The reason for this change is the spread of Christianity and the permeation of politics by religion. The sociology of this semantic change is, of course, quite easy to understand: it is the imposition of a new value system, the total permeation of secular society with this new value system, which transforms the oppositional into the heretical; the enemy could not be tolerated since he not only polluted the faith but also could act as the focal point of opposition. Similar situations arise whenever the integrating element of a society is not primarily a rational agreement among its members, but a new religious or semi-religious faith. The very last chapter of Rousseau's *Social Contract* entitled "Civic Religion" is the modern variant. There Rousseau insists that his society needs a new civic religion so that a true community spirit may be active. Those who violate the moral principles of the community shall be expelled from it; those who pretend to practise them, but violate them, shall be executed. Robespierre, indeed, under the Reign of Terror practised the last chapter of Rousseau. We shall return to this situation.

But once Christianity had become firmly established, the

[3] G. G. Coulton, "The Death Penalty for Heresy from 1184 to 1921 A.D." in *Mediaeval Studies,* XVIII (1924), 1-18.

medieval intellectual enjoyed an enviable position between church and state, benefiting from the advantages derived from this perpetual conflict, being free to pursue his calling within certain limits of heresy and political dissent, and being a member of privileged, self-governing corporations, able to shift his residence, to carry, so to speak, his social base with him.

A new situation arises with the formation of the nation-state. In this process, two stages may well be distinguished: the establishment of the state machine; and the emergence of a national consciousness. The unifying concept of these two stages is that of sovereignty. It creates a fundamentally ambiguous relationship between politics and culture and thus between the intellectual and the state. State sovereignty implies a radical separation of state and society, of politics and culture. The state appears and is constructed as an institution separate from society, and thus implies the toleration of all opinions not forbidden by law, that is, not directly detrimental to the operation of the Leviathan. But, simultaneously, the Leviathan cannot accept limits on its power. I have elsewhere formulated the basic dilemma of modern political theory:

The problem of political philosophy, and its dilemma, is the reconciliation of freedom and coercion. With the emergence of a money economy we encounter the modern state as the institution which claims the monopoly of coercive power in order to provide a secure basis upon which trade and commerce may flourish and the citizens may enjoy the benefits of their labor. But by creating this institution, by acknowledging its sovereign power, the citizen created an instrument that could and frequently did deprive him of protection and of the boon of his work. Consequently, while justifying the sovereign power of the state, he sought at the same time to justify limits upon the coercive power. The history of modern political thought since Machiavelli is the history of this attempt to justify right *and* might, law *and* power. There is no political theory which does not do both things. The most absolutistic

The Social Sciences · 9

theories (Hobbes and Spinoza) which, at first sight, reject individual rights, admit them, however, through a back door: Hobbes, by transforming the sovereign into a kind of business agent of society with all the power he wants if he conducts his business well, but with none if he fails to secure order and security; Spinoza, by his formula that right equals might, permits any social group that is powerful enough to transform its social power into right, to change from an *alterius iuris* into a *sui iuris*. Locke, the protagonist of right and law, felt compelled to admit the prerogative power authorizing the monarch to act without law, and sometimes even against it, if and when right and law tend to jeopardize the state.[4]

This fundamental ambiguity of modern political theory is manifested in the ambiguous position of the intellectual.

In the first stage—prior to the growth of nationalism—no great difficulties arise for exiles, particularly for those possessing skills (military, administrative, judicial, fiscal) which are badly needed by the absolute monarchs in the organizations of their bureaucratic machines. The early period (fifteenth and sixteenth centuries) and the period of enlightened absolutism are excellent examples for the study of the supranational character of the intellectual who frequently changes allegiances and residences and, if exiled by one political power, is gladly received by the other.

Nationalism, as the legitimizing base of state sovereignty, however, produces the really modern problem. It is this period that has most relevance for us. For the claims of the nation upon its citizens—no matter what theories are advanced to limit its power—are basically boundless. The sole limit is—this Luther saw quite clearly—man's conscience.

It was precisely in this period when Grotius lived that the modern problem arose. It is quite fascinating to study the growth of the claims of the nation upon its citizens.

4 My introduction to Montesquieu, *The Spirit of The Laws* (New York, 1949), pp. xxxi-xxxii.

This was seventeenth-century France, where the French national state was formed during the struggle between Catholics and Huguenots. The sixteenth-century religious wars—ending with the ascent of Henry IV of Navarre—demonstrated that religious affinity and confessional identification superseded national identification. But under Richelieu the situation changed. Almost imperceptibly the claims of the nation-state superseded all other allegiances. This is most strikingly revealed during the famous siege of La Rochelle. The Calvinist citizens of La Rochelle, while entering into a treaty with Charles I of England and thus unquestionably committing an act of treason to the country, declared simultaneously that nothing in this treaty should be so interpreted. Here, in the midst of a religious war—and in contrast to the eight preceding religious wars of the sixteenth century—the claims of the nation were felt to be as strong as those of religion.

The conflict between sovereignty and man's conscience leads in modern society to a new phenomenon which has recently been called "inner emancipation." Four instances may make this clear: Spinoza, the Abbé Meslier, Kant, and Theodor Mommsen. All four shared the rejection of the political order within which they lived and the inability or unwillingness to attack it. Thus Spinoza emancipated himself from all dependence upon the political system in order to lead the life of a philosopher. The Abbé Meslier in the eighteenth century practised throughout his life his profession as a Catholic priest, and only his three-volume testament revealed his atheistic communism. Kant appeared to lead outwardly the life of a Prussian university professor, proud of never having missed a lecture and never having interrupted his routine. Yet in his letters he revealed that he thought thoughts that were revolutionary, but did not dare publish them, adding, however, that he never published anything that was untrue. Theodor

Mommsen's testament,[5] released only a few years ago, reveals the conflict of a genuine liberal with a political system which he loathed; his longing for political activity outweighed his desire for scholarly work. Yet all four cases have one thing in common: all four produced and made substantial and, in Spinoza's and Kant's cases, revolutionary contributions to our knowledge.

In the period of liberalism—to which we all tend to look back as the golden age of the intellectual—the intellectual is a free producer. The free university, the independent newspaper, the system of competing political parties are congenial to the intellectual who lives by the sale of his products in a free market.

In the whole period from the sixteenth to the nineteenth centuries there is for the rebel the possibility of an "inner exile," an "inner emigration." But even if he leaves his country or is expelled from it, he can with relative ease find a new home. There is the court emigration (as we may call it) of sixteenth and seventeenth centuries; there is the emigration of the eighteenth and nineteenth centuries when the free (or "uprooted") intellectuals—Herzen, Bakunin, Marx, Byron—roamed freely.

Yet a new phenomenon occurs within the modern nation-state: the bureaucratization of modern society and, with it, the trend to transform the intellectual into a functionary of society. The role of the intellectual encounters ever-growing difficulties. Julien Benda has indicted the intellectuals for treason to their destiny, has accused them of betraying the very moral principles which made their existence possible. If we forget his moral indictment and concentrate on the sociological analysis, we shall find indeed that the intellectuals become increasingly functionaries of society. The process of bureaucratization extends unquestionably to the intelligentsia. Their Socratic func-

5 English translation in *Past and Present*, Vol. I, No. 1, p. 71.

tion becomes endangered. The intelligentsia thus become the defenders of the status quo. It is this change in the status of the intellectual and the change in the social environment which makes the transfer from one to another national culture so difficult a process.

This trend culminates in the totalitarian state. The totalitarian state—and herein lies the difference between it and absolutism—is not and cannot be satisfied with the control of the traditional means of coercion. It must, if it wants to exist as a dictatorial system, completely control man's thoughts, and it must thus transform culture into propaganda. The systematic degradation of thought is something that few people can withstand. Inner emancipation under such conditions means total renunciation of intellectual activity. Indeed, if we ask: What are the intellectual products of the inner emigrants of Germany and Italy? the answer must be: None. The desks of the inner emigrants were empty. There were no manuscripts written during the dictatorship, hidden in desks and waiting to be published after the overthrow of the totalitarian régimes. This is not said to attack anti-Nazi intellectuals, but rather to explain why there was no intellectual production; why the sole remedy for those intellectuals opposed to a totalitarian régime could be but physical emigration.

From what I said before, it is clear that emigration in the period of nationalism is infinitely more painful than ever before. If the intellectual has to give up his country, he does more than change his residence. He has to cut himself off from an historical tradition, a common experience; has to learn a new language; has to think and experience within and through it; has, in short, to create a totally new life. It is not the loss of a profession, of property, of status—that alone and by itself is painful—but rather the weight of another national culture to which he has to adjust himself.

This adjustment is by no means easier if—as in the case of Nazi Germany—emigration is a relief from an intolerable situation. The hatred for National Socialism did by no means ease the psychological difficulties. Not even, or rather, particularly not of those whom I might call "political scholars," that is, those intellectuals dealing with problems of state and society—historians, sociologists, psychologists, political scientists—who were—or should have been —compelled to deal with the brutal facts of politics. I deliberately say: Specifically the political scholars faced the psychological difficulty; for being political, they fought —or should have fought—actively for a better, more decent political system. Being compelled to leave their homeland, they thus suffered the triple fate of a displaced *human being* with property and family; a displaced *scholar;* and a displaced *homo politicus.*

If we attempt to generalize sociologically, we may perhaps say:

Emigration is eased if the intellectual emigrant can transfer his social base; that is, if the social environment to which he moves has similarities basic to that he has to leave.

Emigration is eased if his old audience is replaced by a new one, similarly constituted so that he can talk and be talked to. (This twin conception has been developed by Hans Speier.)[6]

If we apply these two categories to the five situations, we come to the following results:

If, as in classical Greece, civilization is concentrated in one spot, and if politics and culture are one, emigration by the intellectual will normally lead to an atrophy of his intellectual abilities. He may die an intellectual death.

In the universalist civilization of the Middle Ages the social base as well as the audience were, within limits, identical everywhere. Students and teachers of medieval universities came

[6] In "The Social Conditions of the Intellectual Exile," reprinted in *Social Order and the Risk of War* (New York, 1952), pp. 86-94.

from virtually all countries speaking and writing one language, sharing the same basic values.

During the period of the emergence of the modern state machine those having special, particularly military and administrative, skills could actually demand a premium. Their social base as well as their audience were essentially identical at every court.

The emerging national state makes emancipation of the intellectual difficult for reasons indicated, but permits inner emigration as well as, in the eighteenth and nineteenth centuries, quite free emigration.

For obvious reasons it is with German totalitarianism that we have to deal more concretely. This can be done only through an analysis of the actual situation of Germany and of the position of the German intellectual.

The German intellectual's state of mind was, long before 1933, one of skepticism and despair, bordering on cynicism. The so-called Revolution of 1918 produced two new contending politicial theories: Wilsonianism and Bolshevism. The impact of the contending intellectual forces on Europe, and specifically on Germany, can hardly be overestimated. Wilson's grand theory of self-determination, within and without, a League of Nations to end war, expressed the aspirations of German liberalism and the German democratic labor movement. Lenin's revolution appeared to workers and some intellectuals as a chiliastic deed, a revolution ending oppression, emancipating the individual, abolishing political power.

Both theories lost out. Democracy had already lost because it was so closely tied to defeat. It never acquired that self-reliant buoyancy that it had in Anglo-Saxon countries. German liberalism had been corrupted by Bismarck and had traded freedom for imperialist expansion; German Social Democracy had become transformed into a vast bureaucratic machine, trading social freedom for higher wages. Bolshevism, in turn, had rapidly transformed itself into a terroristic machine which, misusing the philosophy of Marx, was solely concerned with increasing the power of the USSR without, and the strangle hold of the ruling clique within.

In this vacuum, the traditional theories of nationalism, restoration theories, began to dominate again German intellectual and, particularly, university life. The universities became the very centers of antidemocratic thought. Let there be no misunderstanding. I do not consider it the task of universities to preach democracy. In this, I fully stand with the ideas of Max Weber expressed in his famous lecture *Wissenschaft als Beruf* (Scholarship as a Profession). But it is most certainly not the function of the universities to ridicule democracy, to arouse nationalist passions, to sing the praise of past systems—and to cover this up by asserting that one is "nonpolitical."

Let me give you my personal experience. When I came in the spring of 1918 to the University of Breslau, its celebrated economist—in his very first lecture—denounced the Peace Resolution of 1917 (peace without annexation and indemnities) and demanded the incorporation of Longwy and Brie, the transformation of Belgium into a German protectorate, the German colonization of large stretches of Eastern Europe and overseas colonies. The still more celebrated professor of literature, after having paid homage to Kantian idealism, derived from that philosophy the categorical imperative of a German victory, a German monarchy, and substantially the same peace terms. When I came to Leipzig in the fall of 1918, the economics professor thought it necessary—in October 1918—to endorse the peace terms of the Pan German Union and of the General Staff, while the historian proved conclusively that democracy was an essentially non-German form of political organization, suitable for the materialistic Anglo-Saxons, but incompatible with the idealism of the Germanic race. When I transferred to Rostock in the summer of 1919 I had to organize students to combat anti-Semitism openly preached by university professors. When I finally landed in Frankfurt, the very first task with which I was faced was to help protect a newly appointed Socialist university professor from attack—political as well as physical—by students secretly supported by a considerable number of professors.

It is well to realize that these doctrines and practices were by no means preached and engaged in by second-rate professors, but by so-called luminaries of the respective universities. The great tradition of Wilhelm von Humboldt no longer existed. Frederic Lilge, in his little book *The Abuse of Learning,* sketches with accuracy and sensitivity the transformation of German learning.

True, there was an Indian Summer from 1924 to 1930. The Republic appeared to be solid. Revolution, Kapp Putsch, Ruhr occupation, inflation, Hitler's Beer Hall Putsch, Communist uprisings—all this seemed to be past. Wilsonianism appeared to make headway. American prosperity made a tremendous impression upon Germany. "Fordism," as it was called in Germany, seemed to be the solution of all problems. Then came 1930, the Great Depression, unemployment, and the gradual disintegration of the political structure. With this, the restoration tendencies within German university life made themselves more strongly felt, and the seemingly great achievements of the Indian Summer came to nothing; or, rather, produced Nazism.

The intellectual emigration caused by Nazism differed fundamentally from previous ones. One may distinguish four different causes (if one is aware that all four may, and often did, actually coincide within one person). They were political, racial, religious, and moral. Political motivation actually comprised the whole range of German political attitudes from conservative-nationalist to communist.

There thus did not and could not exist a political unity among the exiles. It was secondly a racial persecution, and thus hit a group of Jews, half- and even quarter-Jews who may or may not have opposed the régime. It was religious since Nazism was clearly anti-Christian, although the fight against religion could for tactical reasons never be fully carried out. And finally it was simply moral revulsion against the régime, coupled with the conviction that the immorality of the régime made even an "inner emigration" an impossibility.

Thus there was no similarity to the 1848 emigration, which was entirely political and, being so, was conceived by the exiles to be a mere temporary phenomenon.

But Nazism did not simply change the political system of Germany; it changed Germany. Thus for many, exile either from the very beginning, or shortly thereafter the definitive cutting of the ties with Germany, was a conscious transplantation of one's existence.

I may again refer to my own experience: I spent the first three years in England (1933-36) in order to be close to Germany and not to lose contact with her. I actively participated in refugee politics, besides pursuing post-graduate studies in political science at the London School of Economics. It was precisely in England that I became fully aware that one had to bury the expectation of an overthrow of the régime from within. The appeasement policy of the official ruling groups in Britain, combined with the pacifism of the Labor Party, then in opposition, convinced me and many others that the Nazi régime, far from becoming weaker, would grow stronger, and this with the support of the major European powers. Thus a clean break—psychological, social, and economic—had to be made, and a new life started.

But England was not the country in which to do it. Much as I (and all the others) loved England, her society was too homogeneous and too solid, her opportunities (particularly under conditions of unemployment) too narrow, her politics not too agreeable. One could, so I felt, never quite become an Englishman. Thus the United States appeared as the sole country where, perhaps, an attempt would be successful to carry out the threefold transition: as a human being, an intellectual, and a political scholar.

That this transition has been successful, not only in my case, but in hundreds of others, is primarily due to the United States, her people, and her universities. This is demonstrated by the astounding fact that only a few exiles chose to return to Germany, in spite of the fact that the material and nonmaterial rewards of German universities are, on the whole, greater than they are here.

What were the decisive impressions that an intellectual exile coming to the United States in 1936 received here? There are, I believe, three lasting impressions: the Roosevelt experiment; the character of the people; the role of the universities.

I cannot here analyze in detail what the Roosevelt experiment and the character of the American people meant for us. To the skeptical German, the Roosevelt system meant that the Wilsonianism which had been preached since 1917 was not a mere piece of propaganda, but a reality. It was a demonstration that a militant democracy could solve the very same problems on which the German Republic collapsed.

As impressive, and perhaps more so, was the character of the American people, its essential friendliness, the neighborly, almost comradely spirit. Many have analyzed these traits and sung their praises, and I need not repeat all this. The openness of American society made the process of reintegration exceedingly simple, once one had really made a clean break with Europe, and particularly with Germany.

Yet for a scholar it is university life that counts most

heavily. I said before that the transition from one to another culture seems to be eased if the scholar meets a similar social situation. But are the situations in Germany and the United States similar in university matters? Or are the differences greater than the similarities?

The German scholar generally came under three intellectual influences: German idealism, Marxism, and historicism. All three have in common that they are comprehensive systems of thought claiming to fit every phenomenon into its system. All three express the extraordinary weight of an historical tradition. Thus the thought of German scholars was primarily theoretical and historical—rarely empirical and pragmatic. It makes for skepticism. To the historically thinking scholar, the historical process is frequently the repetition of a previous pattern. Innovations are thus belittled at the expense of the "great historical trend." It may make for radicalism if—as in the Marxian theory—history is believed to operate in a specific direction; and it always makes for a certain rigidity bordering on dogmatism.

The whole theoretical-historical approach is (or rather was) accompanied by contempt for Anglo-American philosophy. I still hear the sneers of my philosophy professor about Locke, Condillac, and Dewey, while Whitehead was treated with silence then as now.

Thus, on the whole, the German exile, bred in the veneration of theory and history, and contempt for empiricism and pragmatism, entered a diametrically opposed intellectual climate: optimistic, empirically oriented, a-historical, but also self-righteous.

The radical difference was apparent not only in the intellectual tradition, but in the actual position of the universities. The German universities considered themselves to be training grounds for an élite—although that élite was constituted solely by a socio-economic criterion and not by intellectual achievements; the American universities were organs of a democratic educational principle—that is, the participation of the largest possible number of its citizens in the benefits of education, the élite training being a mere fraction of the total educational effort.

The German university alleged to be a *universitas*, to teach humanistic principles, but had long become a mere agglomeration of professional schools for the acquisition of professional skills as lawyers, doctors, or high-school teachers; while the American colleges had, as a matter of fact, resurrected Humboldt's principle in their general education courses.

The German university teacher was part of a privileged caste with fairly high pay and extraordinarily high social prestige. The American college and university teacher enjoyed virtually none of these privileges. The German university teacher very frequently considered students as disturbing elements, preventing him from his true calling of *Forscher,* or research scholar. The American college professor is primarily a teacher and frequently even a father confessor of his students.

Thus intellectually and institutionally the differences are and were indeed great, greater possibly than the similarities. The impact of this new experience may go (and has gone) in three different directions:

The exiled scholar may (and sometimes did) abandon his previous intellectual position and accept without qualification the new orientation.

He may (and sometimes did) retain completely his old thought structure and may either believe himself to have the mission of totally revamping the American pattern, or may withdraw (with disdain and contempt) into an island of his own.

He may, finally, attempt an integration of his new experience with old tradition. This, I believe, is the most difficult, but also the most rewarding, solution.

The study of the last attitude can, perhaps, best be clarified through an analysis of the role of the social and political sciences and the function of the social and political scientist, with which I am most familiar.

As I mentioned, German scholarship is characterized by the evolution of great philosophical systems during the nineteenth century and, simultaneously, the critique of these systems: Kant, Hegel, and Marx, on the one hand, and Nietzsche and Freud on the other. Kant and Hegel, however, became rapidly transformed into stereotypes, and their direct influence on social and political thought was ultimately disastrous. The academic influence of Hegel was conservative—the extra-academic (through Marx) revolutionary. Kantianism provided frequently the idealistic cloak for very materialistic aspirations. This seems to be inherent both in his theory of knowledge and in his ethics. In his epistemology, the gap between reason and reality has never been bridged. In his ethics, the stress upon the form and character of his categorical imperative made it possible to raise every concrete desire, no matter how arbitrary, to the rank of a universal law. Thus Hegelianism as well as Kantianism did not feed any progressive stream of thought. Marx and Freud were ostracized by German universities, and Nietzsche's critique of German bourgeois virtues (or vices) was transformed into its very opposite.

Thus the great achievements were in the fields of history and law. Yet neither history nor law can possibly come to grips with the social and political reality—the study of which thus found virtually no place in German university life. Scholarship meant essentially two things: speculation and book learning. Thus what we call social and political science was largely carried on outside the universities.

There was one exception: Max Weber, whose name is known and honored wherever social and political science is taught. Weber's greatness consists in a unique combination of a theoretical frame (although for me of doubtful validity), a mastery of a tremendous number of data, and a full awareness of the political responsibility of the scholar. Yet Weber's influence in Germany was very limited. It is characteristic of German social science that it virtually destroyed Weber by an almost exclusive concentration upon the discussion of his methodology. Neither his demand for empirical studies nor his insistence upon the responsibility of the scholar to society were heeded. It is here, in the United States, that Weber really came to life.

This was not always so in Germany. Once, before 1870, Germany and German universities had and practised political science, and it is interesting to know that the Political Science Faculty at Columbia was founded by Burgess after the model of the German *Staatswissenschaft*. Rotteck and Welcker, Robert von Mohl, Bluntschli, Dahlmann, and particularly Lorenz von Stein, were political and social scientists of rank. Public administration, analysis of political parties, comparative political institutions, the structure of society—all this was taught and investigated by them.

This came to an end with the establishment and consolidation of the German Empire, and merely reflects the abdication of liberalism's political role. German liberals concentrated on the *Rechtsstaat* theory (the state based upon law), meaning that the origin, the creation, of law was no longer a concern of theory which confined itself solely to the definition of the right of the citizens, particularly of his property rights, *against* the state. Political and social science was thus replaced by jurisprudence, where the achievement was indeed great.

Thus, from about 1875 on, the *Obrigkeitsstaat*—the authoritarian element—and the *Rechtsstaat*—the legal element—concerned with mere defense of private rights, rapidly destroyed political and social science. The universities train lawyers to administer the state and to defend private rights; teachers to preach the superior virtues of Germandom; technicians; and the theorist and the historian. The social and political scientist, concerned with the reform of society and of politics, is no longer trained. This radically different role of the social and political scientist is perhaps the great difference which the political scholar encountered.

It is quite impossible to assess the contribution of the German exile to the social and political sciences. The character of the Nazi régime caused—as I stressed—the emigration of scholars of radically different orientation, political and theoretical. Thus there is no comparison possible with the flight of Greek scholars from the Byzantine Empire in the fifteenth century. The extraordinary diversity of European refugee scholars makes it virtually impossible to determine their contribution with precision, particularly the contributions made to social and political science—in contrast to those in the natural sciences and, perhaps, in contrast to certain specialized historical and philosophical contributions such as art history, literary history, etc. The influences are too subtle, too diffused, to be easily identified or measured.

Besides, even before 1933 the intellectual interconnections were close between Europe and the United States in the field of social sciences. The importation of Robert Michels, Vilfredo Pareto, and Gaetano Mosca is not due to the post-1933 immigration. The ascent in the United States of the Viennese school of logical positivism seems also to have occurred independently of the political changes in Germany and Austria. Neither of these trends appears to me quite beneficial, both strengthening the a- (or even anti-) historical and anti-theoretical trends in American social sciences.

Those, however, who like myself have been brought up

in the tradition of the great philosophical and historical systems of Europe, believe that we may have added two considerations to American social science:

First and foremost, a note of skepticism. To me, and to many others, the extraordinary optimism about the potentialities of social science to change the world cannot be shared. Our expectations are far more modest; the limits to social science presented by the historical process are far narrower.

There is secondly an attempt to put social science research into a theoretical framework. To many of us it appeared and still appears that the significance of the collection of empirical data is overstressed—as against the theoretical frame; that the predominance of empirical research makes it difficult to see problems in their historical significance; that the insistence upon mastery of a tremendous amount of data tends to transform the scholar into a functionary; that the need for large sums to finance such enterprises tends to create a situation of dependence which may ultimately jeopardize the role of the intellectual as I see it.

These four dangers may perhaps be overstated. But they do exist: The refugee scholar, coming from a different tradition, ought to attempt to minimize their dangers by bringing to bear his theoretical knowledge and his awareness of historical connections. From the outlines of Professors Peyre and Panofsky, I see that they too share my view.

But perhaps more important is that we have received from this concern of American political and social science the demand that scholarship must not be purely theoretical and historical, that the role of the social scientist is the reconciliation of theory and practice, and that such reconciliation demands concern with and analysis of the brutal facts of life. This deepened understanding of the role of social and political scientists, this the United States has given me.

The German scholar returning to Germany for a visit is invariably drawn into the great debate on German university reform. Little has been done to reform the spirit and institutional structure of the German universities, little to change the curriculum. There still exists the deep gulf separating students and teachers; there still is lacking a truly general humanistic education; there still is no evening university; and political and social science is still a very tender plant. But the little that has been done is in large measure due to the example (not the carpetbagging) of returning refugees and other American visitors: their informality, their concern with students, their much greater concern with the political and social reality.

Invariably the returning scholar finds himself in a strange position: While here at home he frequently has to fight the overenthusiasm for empirical research, and to stress the need for theory and history, in Germany he becomes, by compulsion, an advocate of empirical research. It is this dual role in which I see today the true significance of the once exiled German political scholar.

Let us return to the beginning. I pointed out that, in view of the changed external situation of the intellectual and in view of his changed role, exile was an extremely painful experience, and fitting into the new cultural environment an extremely difficult task. Yet I ended by stressing how relatively easy it was to make the change here in the United States.

That it was so easy is entirely due to the American people, its generosity, and its friendliness. No other country has, in so short a time, absorbed so many intellectuals. This is perhaps the place to pay homage to those persons and institutions who have helped to place not less than 520 exiles:[7] Dr. Stephen Duggan and Miss Betty Drury of the Emergency Committee in Aid of Displaced Foreign Scholars; the great foundations—Rockefeller and Carnegie; the Rosenwald Fund; the many private organizations; the churches; the Society of Friends; and the colleges, universities, and research organizations.

Even more important than the financial assistance, however, was the willingness of the colleges and universities to take the risk of employing us, the friendliness with which we were received, and the almost total absence of resentment.

It is these psychological elements that have succeeded in transforming a tragic problem into a happy solution.

[7] *The Rescue of Science and Learning* (New York: Macmillan, 1948).

The Study of Literature

HENRI PEYRE

I

It would be sheer hypocrisy to deny or to ignore the implications of the title and subject for this general series of lectures: one is forced to talk about oneself and to generalize from a personal and inevitably limited experience. For one's experience in a new country, one's adaptation to it, and one's influence on it are bound to depend largely upon a personal equation, which had better be stated frankly, if humorously and gracefully, so as to eschew the naïve egotism of those who are accustomed to having the youth take notes at their feet on each of their dicta. Yet, and in spite of our mild resentment whenever we are considered by others as typical of our native country and therefore as less unique than we should like to be, only those of our reactions which may be taken to have been shared by a number of others in similar circumstances should be stressed as embodying a valid body of reflections on American culture by a half-naturalized European. The lecturer's assumption that he is for a few hours "the Frenchman" vying with Fernandel's expressive mimicry must thus be forgiven. So must the broad claim that his specific title, "The Study of Literature," seems to put forward. Let it be recalled once and for all that America, because of its geographic immensity, of its varied ethnic background, of the utter lack of standardization which prevails in the field of education as contrasted with European countries, offers a number of exceptions to any general assertion which one may venture.

Another word of warning should be in order. The two obvious pitfalls open before anyone who writes on America are fulsome praise of everything American and systematic disparagement of all that is not sufficiently European (hence cultured, refined, mature, spiritual) on this continent. Those same pitfalls have always been laid before anyone who wrote on any country, young or old, and the most common of all complexes in nations is doubtless the inferiority-superiority complex. If touchiness is a feminine prerogative (but women are too generous to have kept it to themselves), from ancient Greece to Russia, from Iran to France and Argentina, all nations have always been feminine, as the gender for the word nation in most languages well indicates. Plutarch relates somewhere the fate of a philosopher, not too remote from a sophist, by the name of Callisthenes. He was asked to deliver an oration in praise of the Macedonians and did it with such a flow of eloquence that all who heard it rose from their seats to applaud. Alexander, however, remarked, quoting Euripides:

> I wonder not that you have spoke so well.
> 'Tis easy on good subjects to excel.

And he ordered him to display the true force of his eloquence by telling his Macedonians their faults, "that, by hearing their shortcomings, they may become better in the future." So did Callisthenes, who was later thrown into prison by the King and put to death.

America has withstood an inordinate mass of criticism, much of it acrimonious and derogatory, for she has served as the subject of some of the best books ever written by foreign observers (Tocqueville, Bryce, Siegfried, Jean Prévost) and of many of the silliest travel books. Her own literature is today more relentlessly self-critical than any other. Her consciousness of her power is now keen and sobering enough to make her lenient toward those critics who may be envious of her or disappointed in too lofty expectations. She is now an old country, or at least a mature lady who has received enough tributes to be inured to vain flattery. The very idea for this series of lectures, which was a timely and an original one, offered a challenge to scholars from whom devotion to truth, sense of proportion, fairness as well as gratitude to their adopted country, and desire to serve it further through constructive criticism are naturally expected.

The question about which five representatives of varied fields of science or scholarship have been asked to do some soul-searching and a public confession is one on which they, like other men in the same predicament, had been led to reflect occasionally. The adoption of a new language, of novel sets of reference, the abrupt assumption, in middle age, of a new background, of new traditions, of a new relationship with a very different public could have been a traumatic experience. That it has been so in only an infinitesimal number of cases is a tribute to American hospitality and to a profession whose chief advantage is closeness with an ever-renewed youth. Any university bulletin, any table of contents of a learned journal, any list of recipients of fellowships, grants, and honors by foundations includes a substantial number of foreign-born scholars and scientists, and bears eloquent testimony to the continued fertility and to the adaptability of men and women who came to these shores from Europe. Although the peak of that influx has long been passed, many of those newcomers are still in their full productive stage. Their children constitute in many cases a group of "hyphenated" young Americans whose gifts are above the average and who hold the cultural traditions of their families in high respect. They have trained many disciples over here. The extraordinary development of American universities and of American science and culture in the last half-century—an even more remarkable phenomenon than the growth of American power or than the industrial and business progress within the same span of years—is due primarily to Americans. Yet, at a time when mass emigration had stopped, since 1925, the contribution of émigrés who were welcomed here added materially to native achievements and often stimulated them.

Economic, military, political leadership has now been thrust upon this country. The burden was not sought for and is not altogether welcome. Complacency, intellectual security, reliance on one's self alone, isolation in relation to "old countries" and very old continents aroused by revolutionary impulses can no longer be practised. But no evasion is possible. The United States must assume the legacy of the Western World and carry that legacy still further: for nothing is safely preserved that is not assimilated and expanded. In doing so, she will rely upon the continued assistance of foreign-born intellectuals who may have not higher, but other, gifts of imagination and of spirit, and know which of those gifts can be used to advantage by an eager and dynamic country, anxious to save the world as well as herself. History will leave it to the credit of the United States, of Canada, and of Mexico that, better than other nations of the New World, they knew how to attract, retain, utilize, and develop energetic and gifted émigrés from a war-ridden continent.

The intellectual migration to America during the years 1925-50 or so may well rank one day as one of the very important migrations of history—not in terms of numbers, of course, but for the debt contracted by a few to many and as an invaluable contribution made by those few to the collective being of which they soon became part. It would be a boon to posterity if more of those émigrés (poets, painters, musicians, thinkers, teachers, political refugees, etc.) would write their memoirs, as Albert Guérard and Vladimir Nabokov have done, and would record their experience in their adopted land. Thomas Mann, Albert Einstein, Darius Milhaud, Marc Chadourne, Giovanni Borgese, Salvador Dali, Jorge Guillèn, W. H. Auden, Igor Stravinsky, Henri de Kérillis, Heinrich Bruening, a score of other eminent names, and a hundred or more distinguished academic scholars could for once compete on a similar theme and leave precious documents to the social historian. On similar migrations in the past we have ample and yet inadequate information.

Without going back to the Greek intellectuals who civilized "uncouth Latium" and made Lucretius, Terentius, Horace, and Virgil possible, or to the handful of scholars who may have left Constantinople after the Turks seized the city in 1453, we may throw a quick backward glance on the first great intellectual migration of the modern world: that of the French Huguenots during the seventeenth century and especially after the Revocation of the Edict of Nantes in 1685. William Penn was one of the first to realize how valuable the Huguenots would prove to his colony, especially as weavers and growers of vines. He was also aware of the high cultural level which had been attained in France by those Huguenots, who belonged almost entirely to the middle classes and had displayed marked intellectual curiosity as well as independence of views. The role of the Huguenots in Prussia, in Holland, in Great Britain, and in America has been explored in several of its facets (the volumes on Huguenot emigration to America by Charles Baird and Gilbert Chinard are well known) but never yet surveyed in a comprehensive treatment: to them the modern world owes its good dictionaries, grammars, and translations, a sturdy blossoming of periodicals, the dawn of a new literary cosmopolitanism, and a powerful impetus to the nascent spirit of Enlightenment.

The second great cultural migration also started from France and caused many members of the nobility to flee to all parts of Europe and to America after the great upheaval of 1789. It is much better known, thanks to the research of Fernand Baldensperger. It gave teachers of languages, of fine arts, of good manners to Europe; more particularly journalists, essayists, and novelists to Germany (Rivarol, Chamisso, Charles de Villers); and sent a few gastronomes, speculators, and enthusiasts of primitive culture to America. But it altered France even more profoundly than it did the countries which provided hospitality to those émigrés fleeting the consequences of the French Revolution. For the exiles from the French nobility and from the upper middle class, frightened by the Parisian mob in turmoil, had to substitute solitude for society life, regret of the past for their former Epicurean enjoyment of the present; melancholy filled their souls, and an unquiet sensibility, prone to seeking comfort in religion, took the better of their former mode of life which had stressed the senses and the intellect; they became receptive to a new literature which had not submitted to analysis and to classical rules or standards but had celebrated passion, death, search for all that was vague and infinite. The majority of those émigrés returned to France, having learned little politically, but as one of them, Chateaubriand, well said in his *Memoirs* and as the remarkable study of Baldensperger was to confirm, having changed inwardly so much that they made the Romantic movement in France possible and provided a public for the writers of the new era.

The nineteenth century witnessed tremendous demographic upheavals: colonial expansion to Asia and Africa, the winning of huge segments of non-European population to Christianity, the settlement of an ever-growing number of Europeans in North and South America. Few of those migrations, however, may be said to have been predominantly intellectual or cultural, with the possible exception of the German liberal migration following the failure of the Revolution of 1848. The large mass migration to America between 1880 and 1924 brought agricultural and industrial workers, pioneers and adventurers, oppressed ethnical minority groups from Russia, Austria-Hungary, or Ireland, but relatively few intellectuals as such. The present century, however, was to be, as Nietzsche had prophesied, an era of revolutions, and those revolutions were to be the most relentless of all: ideological revolutions. Such civil wars as the Crusade of the Albigenses or the Inquisition, even as the American Civil War and as the Spanish struggle of 1936-38, or as World War II which superposed a war against Nazi Germany over a civil war between Right and Left in every country and over a war of colored people in Asia and Africa against the white colonial rule, are fought without mercy until unconditional surrender is obtained. For passions of the spirit are the fiercest of all. Dictatorial and revolutionary régimes similarly single out spiritual and ideological dissent as their primary foe; anything which is not rendered unto Caesar is in their eyes to be eradicated as the most noxious of all weeds, that of heresy.

The era of revolutions which was heralded by that of Lenin in 1917 is therefore marked by the persecution of intellectuals and the exile of many of them. From the Russian emigration which followed 1917, France and America have profited most, France particularly since Russian thinkers like Berdiaeff, Russian writers like Irene Nemirovski, Henri Troyat, and Zoë Oldenbourg seem to have become most easily acclimatized there, as had earlier Polish men of letters and Lithuanian poets like Milosz,

one of the finest in French recently. But as years drew on
and Fascism, then Nazism, appeared as a mortal threat to
free culture in Europe, America became the haven for
intellectuals. The incalculable consequences of the migration to the United States between 1933 and 1950 cannot
yet be described.

Germans and Austrians, especially those who were early
in danger in their native land because of their Jewish
origins, naturally predominate in this influx. They constitute one of the most vigorous elements in present-day
American intellectual life, around periodicals like the
Partisan Review and *Commentary;* they have brought
their methods, their concern for intellectual values, their
capacity for productive work to many departments of
German, of Romance Philology, of Political Science, of
Art, of Economics to American universities. In many respects and in spite of some mishandling of the English
language which in American economics, political thought,
and criticism has today lost all kinship with the elegant
prose of Adam Smith or of John M. Keynes, of Richard
Hooker and Walter Bagehot, of Hazlitt and Virginia
Woolf, those exiles from Germanic lands have enabled
American speculation in many fields to leap forward with
unheard-of boldness. American pragmatism and fondness
for factual empiricism were strengthened by the Germans'
patience for the collection of data and their "Sachlichkeit."
At the same time the other facet of the German mind, by
which it suddenly throws a challenge to the respect for
minute data and embarks upon systematic speculations, is
mirrored in American culture. Philosophy has invaded
many academic curricula; psychological or sociological
generalizations fascinate college youth. Tocqueville had
wisely remarked that "the Americans are much more
addicted to the use of general ideas than the English."

In several respects, American intellectual life is today closer to the German than to the British.

Next to the immense contribution of the German exiles, but surprisingly far behind it, considering the community of language and of tradition, has been the British one. Obviously no compelling force urged the scientists, scholars, and writers from Great Britain to emigrate to the United States. Very few professors from England seem to be called to the English departments of American universities. Some writers decided to establish residence in the New World: Alfred North Whitehead and I. A. Richards have exercised a lasting influence here. The gain in the literary output or to the continued growth of Aldous Huxley or W. H. Auden is more doubtful. Fascism drove but a very small number of Italian intellectuals over here: Enrico Fermi and Giuseppe Borgese are outstanding examples. Many distinguished Spaniards emigrated after the advent of Franco, almost all of them men of letters who have continued writing in their own language, teaching their literature, and living their own culture, with the admirable racy quality which is the privilege of Spaniards. They have not easily been integrated into the broad current of American culture, and their fundamental distrust of efficiency and productivity, of the subordination of the individual to the community and of the family to a broader civic group, hardly prepared them to merge themselves in this country. They have continued developing as Spaniards and as representatives of *Hispanidad*, which is a tribute to the hospitality they received in the United States.

A few features common to these exiles from Western Europe who hailed America as a land of promise may be enumerated: they arrived here fully trained abroad and brought along with them set habits of work, fully perfected methods, pride in their culture and in their past achievement. They were uprooted, in the sense that they were suddenly severed from their countrymen and had no reason to seek close association with foreign-language groups in America or with immigrants from their own nationality who had established themselves earlier in Chicago, Brooklyn, or Cambridge. Many of them were liberals and champions of democracy, but they had little in common with Calabrian peasants, German metallurgical workers, Polish miners, Irish policemen, or French-speaking textile workers from Canada. They were keenly conscious of a cultural past which they missed and which did not make assimilation as easy as it might have been for those who gained immediate advantages from a higher standard of living and a more equal distribution of the comforts of life. Many of them, being artists and writers, or intellectuals in general, were by nature dissatisfied and in reaction against any environment and any way of life which appeared to them as leveling down and as unconcerned with their hyperdeveloped egos. The least adaptable of all seem to have been the artists, and among those the painters and sculptors more than the musicians. There are exceptions, and the names of foreign artists who left Germany after the closing of the Bauhaus school at Dessau come to one's mind: Archipenko, Gabo, Pevsner have settled here from Russia; Duchamp, Ozenfant from France; DeKooning from Holland; Feininger, Grosz, Moholy-Nagy from Germany. But few of those artists have been attracted to the portrayal of the American scene, not even through the transposition into abstract forms which is today their indirect means of representation. Chagall, Léger, Masson, and Lipchitz chose to return to France after World War II. Since then not many newcomers of distinction among sculptors and painters have apparently been drawn to find a permanent abode and a creative stimulus here. Matta Echaurren, Dali, and Ernst had arrived here before 1941.

Frenchmen were once great pioneers, and their epic adventures as fur traders, as missionaries, as soldiers and sailors, even as administrators and friends of native populations hold no mean place in the history of North America, of India and of the Near East, of the South Pacific. Although their country was for centuries the most populated in Europe and double in numbers, if not treble, of their rival Great Britain, they seldom settled in large numbers in their colonies or in the territories which they explored. Their cultural influence abroad was immense; but they could wait for other countries to study their language, their manners, and their art, and to send their own citizens to Paris in search of the refinement, of the *joie de vivre,* and of the pleasant touch of immorality which is supposed to be an ingredient of culture. The defeat of France in 1940 and the Vichy régime drove a limited number of French or naturalized French intellectuals to America. Many of them returned to France after 1944. Complaints against economic and political conditions at home are often heard on the lips of French youth today, and a desire to emigrate to America is frequently expressed. It often remains a mere desire, and the low immigration quota of the French is in fact hardly filled. A sizable proportion of the young men who had been tempted to teach in the United States at the close of World War II has flocked back to France. Not a little of the prestige enjoyed by French people in this country is probably due to their relative scarcity: and the few Frenchmen who are met by the average American belong to the so-called artistic professions: actors, dressmakers, barbers, professors of literature, cooks.

The French have proved more stubborn than most other Europeans in withstanding assimilation. Their resistance to the English language and to the Anglo-Saxon cuisine (as they mistakenly call it, lumping American cooking

with that of England) is proverbial. Both in French Canada
and Louisiana, to a much lesser extent in New York and
in Hollywood and San Francisco, the French have kept to
themselves and to their own cultural traditions. The chief
motive which impels French people to live or to remain
abroad seems indeed to be the delight afforded by the
daily criticism of the strange eating, loving, drinking, and
reading habits of the foreigners among whom they have
transplanted their irony and their national passion for
conversation. There is a strange mutual fascination between the two peoples, American and French. The shrewd-
est analysis of the United States has repeatedly been that
made by French observers, and the appeal of France and
of French literature and art is still unequaled in this
country. But the intellectual migration from France remains but a trickle, and the first American question before
a Frenchman's candidacy to a position over here is: Will
he like our ways? Will he be adaptable?

The impediments to a marriage of true minds between
the two nations are many: First, some cultural patriotism
or even nationalism, deeply ingrained in the French, and
a persistent inclination on their part to view America as
the land of Fenimore Cooper and Jack London and to find
Americans most genuine when they act (at least in their
novels) as primitives greedy for violence. Then the inveter-
ate French habit of critically observing the wines and
the women of foreign lands, and their stubborn conviction
that if a man washes dishes in his home and works too
hard at his office, he has been turned into a slave of a
perfidious matriarchate and is reduced to a tool pouring
gold and his man's brain and his tender male heart into
a crucible to pamper to woman's caprice. Some profound
semantic misunderstandings separate the two civilizations:
The word "leisure," for instance, and even the word
"loitering" (*flâner*) are sacred to the French and to the

Latin peoples generally, while even the most arduous workers among them refuse to proclaim the gospel of work and
to present each of their activities as a service to the community. At the bottom of their hearts they protest against
the condemnation of their first ancestor by a wrathful God
who doomed them to eat bread in the sweat of their brows.
To admit that a country which has no outdoor cafés can
be civilized requires from them a painful stretch of their
imaginations. The Americans, on their own side, will not
easily concede that French is not necessarily synonymous
with Gallic, hence charmingly but deeply immoral. For
many years, in the nineteenth century, a prejudice opposed
anything French as smacking of Catholicism and of popery.
The suspicion against Catholicism has not altogether died
out as France has supposedly become the country of free
thought and of existentialist atheism. Strangely enough, it
is most prevalent among all but the most intellectual circles
of American Catholicism. Only the name "Huguenot" has
continued to be regarded as a fetish, and to give oneself
out as a descendant of the French Huguenots (who, by
that criterion, must have been more prolific than polyga-
mous patriarchs) is a claim to nobility, to morality, higher
than to be descended from one of William the Conqueror's
knights.

The French Protestants, who are such an infinitesimal
portion of the French nation today (probably one-fiftieth
or so) have always been more attracted to Anglo-Saxon
culture than the rest of the country. Some of their Sunday
School stories, many of the novels which are allowed them
in their teens, are translations from the English and pre-
sumably safer than French books for their faith and their
morality. Their curiosity is thus drawn toward "the big
mysterious island," as Proust called England. A significant
proportion of the professors who subsequently seek or
accept positions in American colleges are therefore French

Protestants. Such were Albert Guérard, Fernand Baldensperger, and André Morize among those who recently retired, Louis Cons among the departed ones. Such are several of the present holders of academic positions in French in this country.

The author of this chapter himself grew up in the Protestant faith, was attracted to the study of English and of comparative literature after an earlier specialization in the classics, and first came to America in 1925 to teach in a renowned women's college. No compelling exterior reason, then or since—racial, political, or ideological—drove him to America. He had not even robbed a bank, killed a man in duel or eloped with the wife of his employer, as used to be the case, or the legend, with the black sheep in French families who occasionally disappeared to tempt fortune in the New World or in one of the African or Oceanic colonies. He had not even nurtured an American myth, as many a French adolescent has or still does, whom an inordinate passion for movies, jazz, E. A. Poe, William Faulkner, or Henry Miller has lured to this country in the last three decades. He would in all honesty be at a loss to state the reasons for his first American experiment, and they are immaterial.

But once in this country and plunged first into an ocean of women, then into a very masculine academic community, he tried to understand it from the inside. While most Europeans seldom attempt to penetrate beyond their three poles in New York (Harlem, Chinatown, and Rockefeller Center), beyond the burlesque shows in Philadelphia and Boston, Poe's grave in Baltimore, the Chicago stockyards and, of course, Sunset Boulevard, it was his good fortune to work in America, to be immediately impressed by the qualities of his students, the kindness and intelligence of his colleagues. He read the essays in which apprentices treated the French grammar with a refreshing lack of deference but expressed a vigorous personality. He promised himself he would never write a book on his American experience, so that he did not have to stress the differences unduly and he could thus meditate on the many points of similarity between Americans and Europeans. To be sure, he kept shy of milk and mint sauce and vitamins and mayonnaise and fruits on his salad, but rejoiced that others could like such delicacies while he could be spared them by alleging a mysterious allergy. He looked bewildered whenever the sport metaphors were used by staid old gentlemen, and to this day remains puzzled by homers and first base and gridiron imagery almost as much as by that other invincible barrier separating Americans from continental Europeans: parliamentary procedure and the phraseology of committees. He did not speculate profusely, like his compatriots, on the alleged tyranny, dryheartedness, pride, and demoniacal greed for culture of the American woman. He merely observed, accepted, and liked.

After an American experience of seven years, he returned to his own country where he had intended to make his career. He taught there and in several other parts of the world, compared, and in 1938, again with no compelling motive and not even sensing the ominous catastrophes which were to befall Europe, partly because he was attracted by material advantages and partly because he had retained excellent memories of American youth, he accepted a flattering offer to come back to this country. He has been here ever since, and his adoption of the United States may at least be said to have been a free one, based upon comparative experience elsewhere and a cool estimate of pros and cons. The decision to teach, and to speak and write, and otherwise to pursue his career in this country has never been regretted. In no country that he visited has the writer of these lines found more good will in audiences and among students, more alertness, more seriousness and, to use the one word so dear to the French, more intelligence. Native gifts may have been cultivated more sedulously elsewhere and have been strengthened by more critical training, but nowhere are they in fact more plentiful or more promising.

II

The personal equation thus stated may now be forgotten, and the more general factors, both material and spiritual, which brought or detained foreign scholars and educators over here in the last few decades may be analyzed with some objectivity. Adverse factors in their experience will not be omitted, but favorable ones clearly prevailed and will be stressed as in all justice they should be.

Scholars are less prone than other groups of newcomers to America to wax rapturous over mechanical devices and some of the advantages of comfortable living which may also prove to be the foes of their one real need: silence and some capacity for solitude. The material facilities enjoyed by a literary scholar in particular do not rank with those which may fill with delight an atomic physicist, an electrical engineer, a voracious consumer of diagrams, curves, guinea pigs, and Rohrschach tests. The advantages found in this country by the historian, the philosopher, and the literary scholar are nonetheless real ones, and they contrast, for the newcomer especially, with conditions in shabby and impoverished Europe.

The excellence of American libraries needs not to be praised once more. They are spacious, relatively dustless, well lighted, and they are run not for jealous and forbidding librarians, but for readers. Books are brought to the reader with dispatch and courtesy. New volumes are bought at his request. Photographs, microfilms are readily provided. Catalogues actually include all the books stored, and do justice even to the last letters of the alphabet which in other countries seem to strain the endurance of cataloguing departments. Librarians are competent, zealous, and smile intelligently to the awkward or absent-minded scholar. Libraries are indeed so excellent that the average American does not buy books and often cannot even conceive that books might also be read outside libraries, in his very home.

Research is also appreciably facilitated by assistants and secretaries. Data are compiled, bibliographical information is collected or verified for the scholar; trained secretaries type his manuscripts, point out grammatical or stylistic slips, gently persuade him that consistency should be his primary virtue and that contradictions are not merely, as Emerson called them, the hobgoblin of little minds but the foe, pitilessly hunted out, of those most logical of beings, women. The printing and editing standards of American presses are considerably higher than in several cities of Europe, and an author cannot but be flattered by the respect thus paid his prose.

Even more valuable to the émigré scholar teaching in America is the freedom which accrues to him from his new surroundings. The freedom to move from one university to another is greater than in Europe; offers are readily made, with increased bids, by rival institutions; invitations to lecture are lavishly extended. More important is a certain freedom from solemnity and hierarchy. One is relieved from pronouncing elaborate formulas of address to an Excellency, a *Hofrat,* or *Illustrissimo Direttore.* The custom of calling his new colleagues, after a few weeks, by their first names or even by their nicknames or some mysterious abbreviation of their first names does not make for clarity in social contacts; it is nevertheless, if not overdone, a mark of cordial simplicity. The foreigner is even more pleased to discover that a chairman does not dictate orders, indeed that he listens to others, accepts contradiction from committees that he has appointed, and refrains from placing himself above the law or above parliamentary procedure. Some loss of dignity in academic life may be entailed. Professors do not necessarily wear dark garb and solemn hats and decorations. Students do not bow to them on the stairs; but they treat them with cordiality and frankness. They put to them their naïve queries, and expect them to listen to their confessions and to solve their problems. An outward rejuvenation is often observed among European *chers maîtres* adopted by America. They soon discard the ponderous gravity of one who used to profess rather than teach, and display those flamboyant ties by which American men flaunt their Puritan heritage and proclaim their joy in living.

The first enthusiasm of the foreign-born scholar for the freedom and informality of American academic life soon wears off. Some disappointment often ensues, before deeper values are appreciated. The intellectual in Continental Europe was surrounded with a more refulgent halo, and his vanity was flattered. He had only a modest share in the goods of this earth, since they should rightfully go as a solace to those who cannot enjoy the pleasures of the spirit. But in a stratified society he held an enviable rank. He was the heir to the medieval cleric or to the Renaissance humanist. He was invited by high officials or by ambassadors, consulted by fine ladies on what to read or what to think of what they should pretend having read. Articles by men of letters and by professors were printed on the first page of newspapers, and carried weight with the public. Several European countries had been governed by professors whom the Spanish or French intellectual had known at the University, and he could hope some day to emulate Herriot, Daladier, or Bidault, who had passed from a scholar's chair to the Premier's seat. Students hardly dared disturb him, and office hours were almost unheard of in Europe. Colleges existed for the sake of the professors there, and students were but an adjunct which had to be put up with, unlike America, where professors were expected to serve the pupils and respect in them the potential alumni.

No such reverence for intellectuals prevailed in the New World. Workmen, shopkeepers, insurance agents would bluntly ask the professor how much money he made, and fail to conceal their pitiful contempt at the answer. His pride could not easily take refuge in other standards, since financial values were the prevailing ones around him. Unconsciously, the American intellectual (the artist and the writer suffer far more acutely than the professor from this condition) is driven to emulate the businessman, who sets the standards and represents the norm of the successful person. He dresses and talks like him, answers letters dutifully like him, spends long hours at his office surrounded by three telephones and two dictaphones, aims at efficiency, haste, and productivity.

The American attitude toward culture is healthier than that of the Renaissance, which idolized mediocre humanists, or than that of the French, who pry into the private life of Gide, Cocteau, or Sartre, and deem a pronouncement by those men more momentous than a declaration by Stalin. Still it betrays a fundamental distrust of culture as integrated with life, at a time when cultural values are essential in a war of ideas. When in 1952 the Russian press asserted vociferously that Leonardo da Vinci and Victor Hugo had been precursors of Communism, it paid culture the renowned compliment which vice, said La Rochefoucauld, bestows upon virtue and which goes by the name of hypocrisy. Specialists of propaganda have apparently overlooked the use to which names such as E. A. Poe could be put abroad. Railroad directors might well call one of their trains leaving daily a university town "The Professors" as against five or six termed "The Bankers," "The Merchants," or "The Legislator." Among several thousands of fancy names given to Pullman cars all over the country, why does not one find that of some literary heroine or hero, Daisy Miller, Roderick Hudson, Billy Budd, The Great Gatsby, or Temple Drake? Among streets monotonously called Market, Chapel, Church, Commerce, Meadow, would it be excessive to dedicate some to Thoreau, Walt Whitman, Mark Twain, Eakins, Winslow Homer, and to christen some college halls not only after their donors but occasionally after the scholars who educated the donors and the donors' sons?

No jealousy is felt toward the man of affairs who is the hero of American life (though hardly of American fiction) who, like the French bourgeois under Louis-Philippe, consents to be ridiculed by caricaturists, poets, and social reformers so as to enjoy undisturbed the one pursuit that is truly dear to him: that of power, or perhaps that of perpetual work. In other lands, the poet or the artist used to be portrayed as the cursèd one, trampled upon by society and ruining his health and his normality to offer himself up as the expiatory victim for the *profanum vulgus* whose unacknowledged legislator he was. In America, the man of affairs is the architect of the managerial revolution, the scapegoat for society, the visionary of the future. One of them, at a conference where American businessmen tried to invite their European colleagues to play their parts as martyrs, was reported by the London *Economist* of December 15, 1951, to have gravely stated:

The American manager . . . has more ulcers and more heart involvement per capita than any other class of the American people and he is considered by insurance companies a questionable risk. This may be pretty hard on him, but the results have been very satisfactory for the nation as a whole.

But the intellectual in the modern world stands in need of one commodity above all others: leisure. The very name of leisure meant "school" among the Greeks and has given the word "scholarship." A most learned and painstaking German writer, Friedrich Schlegel, in an enraptured prose idyl, praised idleness as the finest attribute of the gods. Productivity is a very dubious ideal to be proposed to men of thought and to educators. It encourages quantity at the expense of quality and depth. It has lately sacrificed the slow maturing of young men to the temporary need of industry for engineers and salesmen. At a time when the amount of learning and of skill to be acquired by young men is incomparably vaster than ever before, when sciences interlock on all sides and pose highly complex problems to bewildered individuals, when any political or economic move has to weigh the possible consequences it may entail for three continents instead of the three or four countries which alone counted two centuries ago, higher education should reasonably be spread over one-tenth at least of adult life, and life expectancy has grown considerably. Four years in college are no longer adequate. Yet a misplaced standard of efficiency has led hurried educators to sacrifice the quality of the nation's training to speed. Many of the mistakes of our time have been committed by men of good will and of blind devotion to their work who, carried away by the comforting delusion that hard work can take the place of other achievements, lived in a state of nervous tension under which they collapsed. The sad end of most devoted public servants such as a former ambassador to London, a Secretary of Defense, a score of statesmen and envoys, is a gloomy reflection on a way of life which produces goods, but consumes men. The duty of intellectuals and educators is to maintain the validity of their own standards against the drive of a surrounding society which tends to assimilate them to producers of merchandise. By stepping aside occasionally, thinking their problems anew, keeping their nerves relaxed, and bearing in mind the sad statement of Ruskin (who should have known) that "no great man ever stops working until he has reached his point of failure," intellectuals can best serve their country and suggest new ideas and imaginative solutions to our fagged brains dulled by the narcotic of unceasing toil.

While these are real drawbacks, they are not sufficient to offset the spiritual advantages which the refugee scholar gains in America. For while the material benefits mentioned above (higher salaries, better or more spacious buildings, ampler research and library facilities) are very real, they are not in most cases the factors which have lured or detained here the foreign scholars who were not driven out of their native land by force. During a stay of several years in Europe after he had become accustomed to the greater comfort and brighter promotion prospects of an American career, this author for one must acknowledge that he hardly missed the material advantages afforded by America. Indeed he had rather a lurking fear of the perils of intellectual comfort and of the excessive kindness of American audiences which uniformly greet a foreign lecturer with disarming stock phrases such as "It was most stimulating" or "It was a wonderful challenge" or "You have given us an inspiration." The role of excitement, of stimulant, or of challenge might well after all be reserved to drugs, to cocktails, or to one's husband. There may occur moments of discouragement in the career of a middle-aged scholar, who keeps in mind the need to renew himself and his stock of ideas periodically. He misses the pitiless criticism of his European countrymen, who will harshly take him to task for any slipping from his or from their standards and call him publicly a fool, an idiot, or a doting cretin. Over here such gentle formulas of obloquy are replaced by a polite nod of the head on the part of the dissenting person and a courteous phrase such as "You may have got a point there." Agreeing to disagree is a virtue in political life, but it cuts short the discussion of ideas rather abruptly and sometimes stifles altogether the ideas that one might have developed.

But Europe in the years 1930-40 could no longer serenely afford the intellectual arguments and the intoxicating delight of the give-and-take of sparkling conversation. After the analytical works of the 1920-30 decade, the elaborate and anguished Hamletism of Proust, Gide, Kafka, and Pirandello, the complacent egotism of the generation which had escaped the slaughter of World War I, a new spirit appeared around 1929-33. Poets and novelists then realized that they could no longer enjoy the benefits of a stable political régime and polish their sentences undisturbed in a society threatened by war and by misery. Educators and students of the past were confronted by the eventuality of a collapse such as the world had not known since the collapse of ancient civilization. Europe was torn by internecine feuds and by a lurking civil or social war inside every country. Apathy could no longer be a refuge. Many a European scholar then looked upon America as upon the land where European culture, already robustly grafted and naturalized, could continue to flourish if some cataclysm were to spread ruins over France, Germany, Italy. A similar anguish fills those scholars today. The New World is no longer immune from the threats of atomic warfare; yet it seems reasonable to hope that the legacy of ancient and modern culture could best be preserved here. In any case, the foreign-born professor in this country is often haunted by the thought that the future and the very existence of the world as he knows it will be decided within the next ten or fifteen years; they will hinge upon the youth of this country primarily, or upon the collaboration of that youth

and of the generations then in their forties and fifties
which he may have taught in college. The duty of an
educator of American youth thus appears as one of for-
midable significance: to enable his students to understand
the world around them, to prepare for it imaginatively,
and to develop their capacity for leadership.

Everything around him tends to remind the foreign-
born educator of this sense of urgency. In other countries
and in different times, culture could be pursued for its own
sake, and leisurely. It did not have to serve, and the criterion of usefulness was indeed scorned. Students were
relatively few in numbers and came from a favored social
background; they were seldom tempted to ask what advantage they would derive from a study of Plato or of Virgil.
Such is no longer the case. Even the young men and women
who choose to acquire a liberal education are practically
minded. They want culture to help them live and to have
some immediate relevance to life. They flock to the social
sciences because those appear to them more practical and
factual, and claim to be concerned only with the immediate past and with the immediate future which they
attempt to predict. The challenge is a beneficent one for
the professor of literature. He must learn how to reëxam-
ine the legacy of the past which he had accepted blind-
folded in Europe, boasting of a long line of ancestors whose
heir he claimed to be. He takes to heart Faust's celebrated
advice, when he meditates aloud after the departure of
his famulus:

> Was du ererbt von deinen Vätern hast,
> Erwirb es, um es zu besitzen!
> Was man nicht nützt ist eine schwere Last.

III

The study of literature is probably the domain in which
the accession of foreign-born scholars has been least marked

in the last two or, three decades. For, of all the fields of study, it is the one where style is of the greatest importance, and where nothing can replace the perception of the formal esthetic values which is naturally keener with the compatriots of the author than with foreigners. History of thought and of culture, even history of art, has benefited from a larger influx of European scholars than history and criticism of English and American literature: for the medium of the language is less essential in them. Departments of English in American universities have thus remained the least cosmopolitan of all, and the émigré scholars have, as was natural, been most fruitfully utilized by departments of foreign languages and literatures. Their contribution to Spanish and Germanic studies, to French and to medieval and comparative studies has been significant, at a time when the number of eminent native scholars in those domains was small. It is not certain, however, that the foreign professors thus welcomed in the United States have set themselves with the desirable zeal and promptitude to training Americans who would soon be in a position to succeed them. They may have suffered in several cases from the comforting prejudice that foreign literatures are best taught by natives, and thus have strengthened the American inferiority complex in the matter of foreign languages. Too many of them have complacently taken it for granted that students born and taught in New York or Chicago could never rival the native Parisians, the Spaniards who had imbibed Hispanidad in their infancy along with Spanish wine, olive oil, and a taste for bullfights, or the Germans who had sat at the feet of some revered master in Bonn or Freiburg and had Hegel, Dilthey, and Stefan George, as the phrase goes, in their veins.

Such occasional provincialism in the émigré scholars in America is regrettable and has, in our opinion, proved harmful to their field of study in the evaluation of many Americans. The study of foreign countries and of their literatures as an adequate path to the interpretation of the foreign countries, had become of singular urgency in the United States which suddenly was invested with the heavy responsibilities for world leadership. It should be practised today with more energy than ever by gifted Americans. Those should be free from the national prejudices which have long been the privilege, and the bane, of European scholars, each tending to magnify the cultural uniqueness of his own country, be it Norway or Greece, France or Poland. The dicta of Parisian critics, of Spanish or German literary historians, on their own literature should be duly weighed, but also firmly and respectfully set aside by apprentices of the study of literature in the United States. After all, the Germans have long boasted of a brilliant school of Romance or of Shakespearean scholars, the French of equally brilliant groups of Germanic or English scholars who owed part of their originality to the fact that their methods and their backgrounds were foreign, and made no effort to ape or to echo the native criticism of those literatures. A sad gap in American leadership was revealed during World War II when this country had to resort liberally to German-born and German-trained specialists when it had to organize military government, economic assistance, and cultural propaganda in Germany. The devotion of those anti-Nazi German specialists to their adopted country in the New World was beyond question. But American prestige would have been far better served by an able group of specialists of Germany (and of other countries of Europe or of Asia) who would have been Americans looking at foreign problems with a keener awareness of the American scene and of American moods and needs.

Once again the position adopted by the foreign-born

specialist of literature in an American university should be described without falling into the obvious and opposite extremes of carping and ungrateful criticism or of fulsome praise. There have been a few, a very few Europeans who, filled with rancorous spite at the treatment which had been meted out to them in their native land, eager to please those who had welcomed them over here and keenly conscious of the demands implied in the magic American formula "to fit in," decided to find everything wonderful in their adopted country and to look henceforth with condescension at shabby and unstable Europe. But American cordiality is not necessarily naïveté, and few intelligent Americans who ritually ask the question "How do you like America?" expect or appreciate excessive and probably insincere praise. Derogatory remarks about one's adopted country are obviously out of place if they reflect a negative attitude of narrow-mindedness and the inability of newcomers to enter into a way of life which is only superficially different from their own. They have seldom been uttered by scholars who had worked in this country and had therefore learned to appreciate America from the inside, eschewing the hasty silliness of journalists who wish to entertain or to please their own public and sacrifice the delicate shades of truth to picturesqueness and sensationalism.

The position most truly worthy of a European scholar transplanted over here is, in our eyes, that which respects the differences between the two continents, seeks the originality of each contribution to civilization (that of America, that of Western Europe, not to mention South America, Asia or rather Asias in the plural, Russia), and conceives his own role as that of intermediary between the country of his birth and that which he has subsequently adopted. It would be foolish of a European, even of one who has suffered in his native land, to repudiate the culture which molded him and to misjudge the intellectual and spiritual forces which still make Europe the most creative continent. At a time when America is expending money, machinery, men, and her confidence in Western Europe to preserve it not only as a fortress or as a bridgehead but as a bastion of civilization, it is fitting for an Americanized European to bear in mind the eloquent statement with which aging Michelet prefaced his volume *Du Dix-huit Brumaire à Waterloo:*

> Europe, they say, is very old. But there is more youth in her apparent old age than anywhere else on the globe. Her living electricity, which makes her highly mobile, enables her daily to renovate herself through the spirit, and the spirit in turn endows will-power with unbelievable strength. Let a great idea appear, will-power weaves and creates a world with it.

Some of the differences between cultural conditions in the United States and in Europe are valuable ones and should be preserved; others can be eliminated through the mutual acquisition by each of what is best, and assimilable, in the other.

The first feature which impresses the literary scholars, like other scholars or scientists transplanted here, has often been described and praised. But it must be briefly recalled in any survey of the subject, for its importance is primary. American academic atmosphere is relatively free from the pettiness that often prevails elsewhere and from the fear of risk and of novelty which grants a premium to routine. There is relatively little envy, and the welcome which has gladly made room for the émigré scholars and has pushed them to top positions would be inconceivable in any other land. A scholar is encouraged to formulate new plans, to propose reforms, and, provided he does so in a coöperative and constructive spirit, he is often greeted with the most beautiful of all American formulas: "Go ahead!" Money is seldom a problem, and it is eventually found. The more gigantic the undertaking, the more extensive the survey and occasionally the bigger the words used by sociologists, psychiatrists, and even by humanists, the readier will the financial response be. At the same time, there prevails a spirit of coöperation which is conspicuously lacking in Europe, where not only scholarship but science also depends mainly upon the individual. Collective undertakings can be carried through far more easily in America than in Europe. Nationalistic bias, social or political divergences do not interfere with the determination to accomplish a task in common. A cantankerous spirit is relatively rare. "Keep smiling" is an advice that arouses a smile on our lips, but it is taken seriously by many. Small colleges have several times been portrayed as poisoned "groves of Academe" and as surrendering to conventionality and cant; but the cordial breadth of mind encountered in most large American universities is an undeniable superiority over the mutual suspicion which prevails in countries where competition is keener and envy rife.

A ransom is to be paid for such good-humored cordiality and spontaneous trust in human nature. Irony is perhaps deficient or is frowned upon as destructive and malignant; for in irony there is iron and the sharpness of a blade, as a great master of language who was an imaginative etymologist, Victor Hugo, once said. Some of the solemn conventions of American oriental orders, some alumni gatherings in which staid if not sober alumni don fanciful garb, some gatherings of learned societies in which strings of abstruse papers are gravely and meekly listened to, amuse the foreign observer, who assumes that all this smacks of the child in man that should be outgrown when one has reached the age of reason. Humor is preferred to irony, and has indeed more charm, because it blends irony with sympathy, a pitiful heart with a keen and amused intellect; perhaps also because it is a means of eluding the tragedy of life, and of smiling in order to conceal or to repress the emotion.

But the critical spirit, which unlike irony is an almost unadulterated virtue if practised with moderation, is not overdeveloped in American students. The first reaction of the newly arrived scholar from abroad is one of relief. In several countries of Europe, and in France in particular, education seems to have been primarily designed to train critics and to teach disbelief. Most of the thinkers proposed to the admiration of the youth were advocates of healthy, methodical doubt: Montaigne, Descartes, Voltaire, Renan, Claude Bernard. The quality of the critical articles in periodicals is strikingly high: the very best minds seem concerned with examining, doubting, weighing, distrusting prejudice and appearances. Audiences at a lecture, at a concert or at a play seldom yield to rapturous enthusiasm. One word punctuates their comments: the little preposition "but." "It could have been a good play, but . . ." or "It was an interesting lecture, but. . . ." The marvel of it all is that such relentless criticism has not hampered creation, that, indeed, it seems to stimulate the writing of books and of music, and that neither lecturers nor actors whose every intonation, every interpretation is scanned by pitiless observers appear to have been discouraged by those Parisians who will not accept on trust a new book or a much advertised film any more than they do a bottle of wine or a fiancée.

Americans are, in contrast, more readily addicted to enthusiasm or perhaps to polite praise of any foreigner who has come from abroad to play his music, expound his ideas, and vituperate against the shortcomings of American civilization. There may be some masochism in them when they meekly buy a ticket for a lecture in which a foreigner will assail their soullessness or their capitalist greed or their philistinism in art, or perhaps merely a fine sporting instinct which makes them shake hands with the vituperative lecturer and declare, "It is good for us to hear such things." But if the visitor from abroad settles here, he soon discovers that, behind the shallow and uncritical reception which is often given him, there is mostly reserve and shyness. If the young American is encouraged to form an opinion of his own and to oppose it to others with convincingness and sincerity, he is eminently capable of having such an opinion and of expressing it with wisdom and brilliance. It has been the frequent experience of many foreign teachers in this country to receive from the better undergraduates papers successfully rivaling the very best written by students at Oxford, at the Sorbonne, or at Heidelberg. The quality of many Ph.D. theses in literature is now easily comparable to the best products from Europe. And if American periodicals do not as yet publish enough critical articles of outstanding merit, it is usually because their editors wrongly believe their readers to prefer any fourth-rate short story to a first-rate critical study. The young men gifted enough to write such critical articles are here, in the universities, and could easily be drawn upon and encouraged.

The French professor of literature is also heard to deplore the lack of training and of skill in writing in American students, and consequently or similarly in American writers. Here again allowance must be made for a different background and a different set of values. America is now becoming a haven for rhetoricians; Kenneth Burke and some of the once "new" critics are unparalleled at the present time in the Old World. But less stress is placed at school on the subtleties of composition, and less effort is made to order one's thoughts in a manner which will both surprise and persuade. Transitions, on which Flaubert and many another Frenchman have laboriously pondered, often leave the American writer beautifully unconcerned.

A young essayist will readily declare at the beginning of a paper, "I enjoyed reading this play of Racine" or "I hate that morbid writer Proust," which in Europe would afflict his professor with an apoplectic stroke or with a sudden baldness. Every third sentence, in written and even in spoken French, seems to be a litotes. The word is almost unknown in America, and innuendoes, even understatements, fail to play the same role of tempering every assertion. "Il n'y a de vérité que dans les nuances": this little maxim of Benjamin Constant is a favorite one with every French teacher of literature, and "nuance" is one of his key words.

Much has been lost with the disappearance of such a refined and allusive way of writing. The genteel and polished essay, such as was long written by English historians, critics, and urbane and humorous moralists, is perhaps the most original and, with due credit to Montaigne, autochthonous form in English letters. Virginia Woolf, G. M. Trevelyan, and Americans who had been profoundly anglicized, Logan Pearsall Smith, T. S. Eliot, have given admirable examples of it in the last few decades. As an art form, that essay is unfortunately on its way out. Our magazines find it too leisurely, too long and rambling, too nonchalant, too subtle. They are swayed by the triumph of a journalistic technique, which affects a more abrupt and more crudely outspoken style and rates "punch," speed, effectiveness above the more traditional qualities of style. We can but mourn the loss. But the shock values which are at present favored by our magazines are responsible in part for the very trend which they deplore in American letters: the premium granted to violence and brutality, and the fear of the intellect in our creative writers, as if they might endanger their precious primitive and "grass roots" virtue if they once started having ideas or analyzing themselves.

The American man has been defined by a Spanish thinker as "a civilized man with no traditions." The definition is of course deceptive; the taste for ancestors' portraits, a passion for genealogy, the hunting of antiques, the restoration of old houses, the naïve appeal of inns where Washington once slept or of houses which Jefferson once visited, the cult of legal precedents, are also American traits. It is probably more accurate to say that the sense of history is less deep and less all-pervading here than it is in Western Europe. The European man is often crushed by the weight of his past. Unable to accept and assimilate the whole mass of it, he elects one period or one trend in that past as worthy of his cult and fights against the rest, and against his compatriots advocating the opposite trend or selecting another century as their utopia. Thus could Hilaire Belloc, an Englishman in whose veins ran some French blood, say that "civil war is a constant function of Gallic energy."

Americans are divided, and their own Civil War was more ruthless than any European revolution. It has left them with a secret but deep complex, a lurking fear of disunity which periodically flares up and is discernible today in their emotional wrath against Communism in their own midst. Their attempt at integrating the millions of foreign-born among them has been inspired in part by that fear, and pushed intelligently and, on the surface at least, successfully. The study of American history has recently been strengthened in many schools and praised as a storehouse of the best traditions which have made the American an individualist, a pioneer, a tolerant and god-fearing democrat. Nevertheless the foreign teacher or lecturer in this country is struck by the frailty of the knowledge of, and of the sense for, history. While most Europeans remain to this day sons of nineteenth-century historicism and tend to explain any phenomenon by its genesis and any movement through its origins and slow growth, the revolt against history is never very far from the American mind. It has been the experience, rarely but occasionally, of a French lecturer in this country to be imprudent enough to invite questions from the floor, and to be startled by the realization that the king who had been described as introducing the Renaissance from Italy into France had been surmised by one as being Charlemagne, by another as being Louis XIV. A naïve but eager traveler he once spoke to on a train seized the opportunity of meeting a Frenchman to clear up a point which had long puzzled him: whether Bonaparte and Napoleon had been two different rulers, or one and the same man. Among better informed and more sophisticated persons, and notably among the adepts of the social sciences, hostility to history has become a set policy. An effort is made to break with the past altogether and to concentrate on what has been observed, classified, and translated into charts and diagrams only since censuses, polls, and elaborately indiscreet questionnaires came into being. Going back more than ten or twenty years in studying social behavior or international relations is frowned upon, unless one jumps determinedly over the previous thirty centuries and explores the artifacts of primitive men and the sexual mores of remote oceanic tribes.

Some freshness is gained thereby. The European man has more than once been hampered by his obsession with history and has failed to envisage new situations as fundamentally new and therefore to propose imaginatively new solutions for new problems. History with him has all too often served to foster nationalistic suspicions, boastful claims, jealousies of other nations. European philosophers of history have often been obsessed with cyclical conceptions of man's evolution and have predicted tragic collapses for our culture on the strength of doubtful past parallels arbitrarily interpreted. Scholarship, understood as genetic study of hypothetical sources and mistaking the previous occurrence of an idea or of a stylistic device as a cause having helped produce the subsequent reëmergence of the device or of the idea, has fallen into blind alleys. Michelet, in 1855, prefacing his volume on the Renaissance, looked back with gloom on the harm which the reign of history was causing his own country:

> History, which is nothing less than understanding of life, was to vivify us; it has, on the contrary, weakened us, making us believe that time is everything, and will power nothing. We have conjured up history, and now it is everywhere around us; we are besieged, stifled, overwhelmed by it. . . . The past is killing the future. . . . In the name of history itself, in the name of life, we must protest. History has nothing to do with such a heap of stones. History is history of the soul, of original thought, of fecund imagination, of heroism: the heroism of action and that of creation.

Nietzsche, in one of his *Unzeitgemässe Betrachtungen*, echoed such a protest when he, trained in philology and history, revolted against the historical intoxication of his age and wanted to substitute *memento vivere* as a motto for the *memento mori* of those who use history as a convenient way to avoid life and action. The blurred or vague historical sense of many Americans deprives them of much pleasure; for the intellectual joy of knowing the past and the poetical halo which transfigures even dull details as they appear in the perspective of the past are a source of enjoyment to the historian. But a certain freshness is also gained. Teaching unsophisticated young Americans can be a rejuvenating experience for a European. Chaucer, Racine, Bossuet, Dürer, Monteverdi suddenly spring alive to his American students, who treat them as if they were contemporaries. Some lovely coeds discover with raptures Plautus or Chrétien de Troyes or some other writer of old who to many a young European had appeared merely as an instrument for his mental torture in some required course. In some respects, the freshness of the happiest of all peoples, the Greeks, who had no ancient or foreign language or literature to study, few previous systems of philosophy, no catechism or dogmas, no chemistry or biology, and could concentrate on poetry, eloquence, art, dancing, gymnastics, and leisure, had been inherited by young American undergraduates. It is, however, fast disappearing.

"Freedom" is another word which recurs on the lips of those who have come over from Europe and praise the hospitable intellectual climate which they have found in the United States. It is, along with "charity" and with "solidarity," the most beautiful of substantives, and those who had suffered from the eclipse of political and intellectual liberty in Europe are most eloquent in singing its praise. The noble word "freedom" may have lost some of its glamour when, in the first decades of our century, Western men, in their secure enjoyment of freedom, had become too sensitive to some of the vulgarizing or leveling effects of democratic rule. But Europe suddenly awoke to discover Fascism, Communism, Hitlerism, and to realize that the disappearance of freedom would be tantamount to the extinction of life. From Pericles and Cicero to Montesquieu, from Locke to John Stuart Mill and Croce, from Shelley to Eluard, passages should be culled which should be proposed as sacred texts for the study of the young in the one world that we like to envision. The present writer may be the least qualified of the authors in this volume to expound the advantages of freedom in America, for he had not suffered from any restrictions to freedom of thought in his native country. He may, however, bear witness to the utmost latitude which has always been granted him in private universities in this country, to think, write, and say anything that appeared to him as true. And he has not refrained, and never has been asked to refrain, from trespassing into the domains of religion, politics, economics, and international relations.

A word of warning may, however, well be in order. Some Americans are fond of assuming that, because there is more freedom in this country and because universities are free from federal supervision, because neither academies nor state-subsidized theatres exist, because (in a sense, at least) the American press is or calls itself free, it necessarily follows that thought, science, and literature are freer in the United States than elsewhere, and intellectual progress more assured. We smile, rightly no doubt but complacently, at Hitlerian anthropology and science under the Nazis, at the Stalinist rebukes to geneticists, semanticists, and musicians who fail to obey the Marxist line. No one wishes to suggest that Nazi or Communist restraints upon science are laudable or beneficent, or that restrictions and more Federal control be established in free America.

But it would be rash to fancy that no good science and no good literature flourished in the past under tyrannical régimes. French science was perhaps, in mathematics and physics, never greater than under the totalitarian rule of Richelieu and of Louis XIV, and the glory of French letters and philosophy then has hardly been excelled. Chemistry, biology, and physics with Carnot, Ampère, and Fresnel shone brightly under the iron rule of the Terror and of Napoleon the First. The achievements of German chemists and engineers under Hitler, those of the Russian scientists today, must not be complacently underestimated. In literature, Goethe, Schiller, Hegel, and a dozen stars of German romanticism illumined the very years when Germany was cringing under Napoleon's scepter. Goethe bowed to every petty nobleman whom he encountered in the streets of Weimar, to Beethoven's disgust, and deemed it an exalted favor to receive the Napoleonic Legion of Honor and to be granted an interview with the Emperor then occupying his country, while Hegel contemplated him, riding on horseback in Jena, as the supreme embodiment of the historical process. Many a neutral observer of Italy when the country was occupied by Mussolini or by the Allies, or of Berlin under quadripartite rule, and of some neighboring free countries in Europe has remarked that "political freedom and freedom of the spirit do not necessarily go hand in hand" (Igor Markevitch, in *Made in Italy*, 1949). Free Switzerland and free and prosperous Holland or Denmark have not necessarily thought, composed music, or elaborated political and social systems with the greatest freedom.

Free discussion is everywhere allowed and encouraged in American colleges. Debating teams ritually, if sophistically, argue the pro and con of every question. Newspapers are fond of printing contradictory reports on many events, and radio time is carefully parceled out to the opposing sides in every important issue. Any professor may theoretically say anything he likes at a faculty meeting, and anyone from the floor may nominate any slate of officers and proclaim his disagreement with the majority or with the administration. But respect for the majority rule and courtesy seem to be so ingrained in this happy land that dissent has become a rare occurrence, at least among academic people. Reverence surrounds any colleague who happens to have been nominated to any committee. Unanimous votes are the rule in those new Edens, college campuses. Student newspapers seldom criticize or even call into question the fundamentals of the education which has been organized for them by their elders. Since the pro and the con can be freely argued by the newspapers and the radio commentators, one listens nonchalantly and ritually skips the editorials. Shoulders are shrugged when a paradox is uttered, even if paradoxes often prove to be the truth of tomorrow or the unperceived truth of today. Theoretical freedom of thought becomes too little conducive to boldness of thought. Facts are presented liberally to newspaper readers, and means of knowledge are abundantly placed at the disposal of university students. But their passive resistance to thinking about the facts is underestimated. A certain lack of adventure in initiating new ideas, in making startling new discoveries, in predicting the apparently unpredictable has been noticed, by Americans themselves, as constituting the Achilles' heel of their culture. Knowing facts is doubtless important; but it is of little avail unless, as Shelley says toward the end of *Defence of Poetry*, "we imagine that which we know."

IV

The greatest tribute that is paid America by the foreign scholar who has made America his home and who looks back with some pride at what he has been inspired to achieve in this country and gives thanks for it, is that he has been able to develop both as a teacher and as a scholar. For, just as his allegiance is to Europe, which had trained him and which he carries with him to his adopted *patrie*, his function is both to train others and to contribute to knowledge himself and pursue his research and publications. This twofold requirement is an exacting one, and it is becoming increasingly hard to meet it, owing to conditions around us. Contrary to the fond assumption of those who visit our Gothic towers and verdant lawns, and imagine that, in an American university, all is *luxe, calme et volupté* (the last, of course, spiritual), we are condemned to wage an unceasing fight to retain the time and the energy necessary for the discharging of one of our essential obligations: to the accumulation and interpretation of knowledge.

In the domain of education, a professor who has, impelled by circumstances or of his own free choice, made his career in the United States may well be proud of having played his part, however humble, in the most impressive educational development of the century. Legitimate disappointment, it is true, may be voiced regarding the schools of this country. Some, in the large cities and elsewhere, are excellent. Many are mediocre. Dissatisfaction with the secondary education that he received is a chronic cause of complaint with the thoughtful American of either sex. Far too little as yet has been attempted to remedy glaring faults. The raw material of America, as we brutally call it, the children, are at least as gifted as in any other country. The best of them manage to achieve, in spite of the handicaps of a schooling of questionable quality, amazing results. Several signs, however, point at present to a slowing down in the rate of intellectual progress in this country. Only a thorough reform of the schools could again enable Americans to forge ahead and to rise up to the expectations that the world places in them: and these are none other than leadership of the world, technical, intellectual, and spiritual. America's chance is here and now. Tomorrow may favor other sections of our planet, for, as the French historian Lavisse used to say, "La faculté de conduire l'histoire n'est point une faculté perpétuelle."

The fallacies from which our educational system suffers are the utilitarian one and a mistaken conception of democracy. Thoughtful visitors from abroad and scholars and scientists established here are unanimous in condemning them; and they do so out of earnest devotion to this country, and not in an acrimonious spirit of disparaging all that differs from the traditions which Europe has inherited from the Renaissance. The utilitarian obsession has blinded many Americans, too many normal colleges and departments of education, too many taxpayers wanting to get "their money's worth" in the form of measurable and immediate returns and in fact encouraging routine and mediocrity. Young men and women must obviously acquire certain skills which they may need in different walks of life. But they would easily acquire those on the job itself, and fairly promptly. The fact is that, in America especially, one seldom stays in the career one had chosen at sixteen or twenty. The chances of travel, military service, of marriage, of friendly or family connections, plunge most young men into work for which they were not particularly prepared.

Consequently some general culture, the ability to exercise common sense or to display sound judgment, the discernment of men which is developed by the study of man in history, literature, and the humanities in general, some personal charm often more marked in a man with a broad cultural training and able to see his subject as part of a larger whole—these are more valuable assets in life than a narrow specialized training. The men who reach the top in their profession, in diplomacy, administration, banking, commerce, are in most cases those who had been shrewd enough not to stress the utilitarian aspect of their training and who, when studying, reading, and listening, had not been obsessed by the naïve question of some crude adolescents (echoed, alas! by some of their educators): "What use will this subject be to me?"

Democracy has been too often interpreted as leveling down and, if envious masses cannot raise themselves to the level of their more fortunate neighbors, they will at least undertake to bring their neighbors down to their own none too exalted standards. Traditional subjects which now pass for aristocratic (the classics, even foreign languages, the arts, a certain variety of vocabulary and polish of style) are being expelled from many schools and even from colleges which train the teachers for the schools. It is claimed that the men of the future need primarily to be adjusted (to a none too perfect society, to be sure) and attuned to the mass and machine age in which they are to live. The educators who have been steeped in a European tradition cannot but think that most of the great scientists, engineers, biologists, in the past were brought up in a humanistic discipline and were not thus hampered from making startling discoveries. They are bound to confess, and many native American scientists have first proclaimed it, that even today many of the most original discoveries in science were done abroad and subsequently perfected here, and that the essential gifts of imagination and of original thinking flourish best in men whose training has not been narrowly circumscribed by one field of specialization. Pasteur was not specialized in medicine, and Claude Bernard began by writing a tragedy. Jefferson, Gladstone, the French Revolutionaries, the greatest American and English statesmen were trained, not in civics and contemporary democratic behavior, but on Plato and Thucydides, on Cicero and on Locke, Rousseau and Burke. It was lately asserted that President Truman wisely knew how to spurn the temptation of a prolonged stay in the highest office because he had learned "American" traditions through the reading of Plutarch's *Lives*. What a nation wants is not necessarily what it needs, and educators should have the courage to make it want what it needs. Leadership is not incompatible with democracy. Indeed, democracy can hardly survive without the continued ability to evolve leadership out of its own midst. The age and the countries in which the study of public opinion polls, of the techniques of propaganda, and of the behavior of men in a machine age have been emphasized in the last few decades have also been the age and the countries in which democracy has been dealt its worst blows. The words of warning which Walter Lippmann uttered in December 1940 are not totally unjust in their severity:

During the past forty or fifty years those who are responsible for education have progressively removed from the curriculum of studies the western culture which produced the western democratic state; the schools and colleges have, therefore, been sending out into the world men who no longer understand the creative principle of the society in which they live.

In a few other respects American education appears deficient to the foreign-born professors, who point out its deficiencies because they believe they could easily be cured, and because they are not fundamental expressions of the American temperament but slippery paths or blind alleys on which this country may have momentarily ventured.

First is the fondness for innovations. It is probably beneficent to correct and perfect a machine, to modernize it with new gadgets, to adorn it with new selling devices. But it is regrettable that our halls of learning should not be a little more impervious to tides of taste or currents of shifting opinion rushing on them from outside. Every winter, to offset their financial inability to indulge in winter sports or to test the sun-burning virtue of the Florida sun, college faculties embark upon their own indoor sport, overhauling the curriculum. Progress is regularly conceived by them as lying in the direction of more complexity, and the deciphering of college bulletins and of the requirements for courses, majors, etc., has now become harder than mastering the riddles of relativity. *Quieta non movere* was also a worthy ideal. We absent-mindedly forget that many of the by-paths into which our fury for educational reforming or rephrasing waylays us had probably been already explored by our predecessors and rejected as leading nowhere.

A second evil connected with the first is our desire, for publicity purposes and for other reasons, to have college teachers produce intensively. There are cases when a gentle outside compulsion may indeed elicit a worth-while article or book from too modest a scholar, who might not otherwise be led to believe that his thoughts are worth printing. Having published one or several books may prove to be salutary hygiene for a professor in the same way that some countries, or some doctors, regard pregnancy as a universal panacea for some of the true creators in this world, women.

'Tis pleasant, sure, to see one's name in print.
A book's a book, athough there's nothing in't,

mocked Byron. We have lately equated productivity with quantity, and much criticism published in learned journals hardly sprang from an irresistible inspiration. One of the wise men of our time, who has known American universities from the inside and has settled in a country which is occasionally severe to academic scholarship in the United States, well said:

If people only wrote when they had something to say, and never merely because they wanted to write a book, or because they occupied a position such that the writing of books was expected of them, the mass of criticism would not be wholly out of proportion to the small number of critical books worth reading (T. S. Eliot, *The Use of Poetry and the Use of Criticism*).

A third and graver evil, from which foreign-born professors in America have been far from immune, is bad writing. We are too prone to assume that we have practised new methods only if we have coined new labels to cover old or newly wrapped merchandise. A scientist hastens to invent a new symbol to designate a new phenomenon or substance. Social scientists evolve an elaborate private terminology, and zealously borrow the outer trappings of science. The contagion has extended to the so-called new critics, who bandy about epistemological jargon and, unlike Roman augurs, seem able to look at one another without laughing. Psychoanalytical jargon has invaded literary interpretation and opened a gulf between needlessly specialized writing and the general public. An American official, Paul Porter, director of the European Coöperation Administration, had the courage to protest, early in 1952, against such a disfigurement of English style perpetrated in the country which had once produced the splendid writing of the Declaration of Independence and of the Gettysburg Address. He denounced "the worst writing of English today, which is surely produced in the United States Government" and the inflationary disease of five-syllable words. The disease has not been confined to Washington.

These shortcomings, which have hampered the growth and especially the qualitative refinement of the study of literature in America, may be traced to the unconscious acceptance of two ideals by academic scholars and critics: the ideals of the businessman and of the scientist. "Efficiency," "punctuality," "productivity," "coöperation," "good fellowship," "service to the community," are words rightly revered by the man of affairs. Since a business career is to most Americans the most enviable one and the one in which it is felt that the country has most conspicuously asserted its supremacy, intellectuals, writers, and artists are tempted to adopt the standards and outward behavior of business life: regular office hours, availability in an office, statistical charts, carbon copies duly filed, prim and respectful secretaries whose main function is to stimulate American wives to perpetual rejuvenation and to sublimate male eroticism through chastened and secure dreams amid filing cabinets. The few hardy souls who resist such methods are the wretched nonconformists who take refuge in Greenwich Village, or along the California beaches, or in drinking or abnormality. The European intellectual sensibly decides to do as others do and to forsake reverie, fantasy, and caprice in his American life. But he occasionally sighs for the original work he might have accomplished in the inefficient lands where letters are not necessarily answered, appointments are irregularly kept, and telephones blissfully get out of order.

The prestige of science has been more bewitching and perhaps more disastrous. Scientists have achieved such results in the last hundred years that others have placidly assumed that only through scientific method would their discipline accede to the august rank of a science, as chemistry and biology had once done. Psychology, sociology have scored undeniable gains thereby. The gain to the interpretation of art and literature is much more doubtful. Exhaustive knowledge, accurate observation, submission to texts, relative and critical spirit, intellectual honesty are virtues usually found in scientists which literary scholars must also possess. Objectivity and impartiality are less undeniably beneficent, and it may well be, as Baudelaire contended, that "passionate partiality" endows a critic with keener insight. But when scientists ask their literary colleagues what are the precise and stable criteria on which they rest their assertions that Balzac is great and Meredith or Dreiser less great, they can only reply that stability and uniformity are in no way desirable in the opinions emitted by varied people of different ages on literary writers.

The study of literature would be even less securely based than it is at the present time if it rested on semantics, psychological measurements, esthetic tests for beauty, etc. For these are even more susceptible to change than the elusive criteria of good taste, penetration, power, intensity, and subtlety. It would be folly for literary study to ask science to provide it with models for stable values at the very age when physics, biology, psychology have been, in a span of fifty years, rocked to their foundations by tremendous upheavals. One thing is well-nigh certain: that the authors and artists of the past who are acclaimed today as great, and even some of the present time, have a strong chance to be considered as great twenty and fifty years from now. But the views held at present by medicine, genetics, physics, anthropology, and psychoanalysis are sure to be rejected twenty and fifty years hence. Our descendants will smile at most of them. "Scientific truth is an error of today," wrote J. von Uexküll in 1909, in *Umwelt und Innenwelt der Tiere,* and he was no mean biologist; and it might equally be asserted that the scientific truth of today will tomorrow be regarded with pity as an outdated error.

V

This paper, begun in a spirit of grateful acknowledgment of the immense facilities for growth encountered by one of many European scholars in his adopted land, may seem to have been diverted into the sanctimonious criticism of a preacher. But it would be a disservice to the country which has bestowed many benefits upon its refugees or émigrés from overseas if we flattered some of its prejudices and did not warn it against setting its goals too low. The intellectual migration from Europe has now subsided: in Germany, Italy, France, and in most countries fortunate enough not to have been screened behind the Iron Curtain, scientists and scholars are again fired with hope for the future and are working steadily to bring about a better future. In America, those scholars and scientists who had migrated here have now become fully integrated into the cultural life; their sons and daughters are American. They may look back upon the achievements of the great country of which they have become part and point out some lag still remaining between the unbounded expectations the rest of the world rests in America and the limitations to which this country seems willing to submit too meekly.

For the intellectuals who have migrated from Europe have a heavier duty to America than devolves upon the average citizen of the United States. The most signal failure of this country, which thinks it has perfected propaganda techniques and mass media, has been its futile attempts to make itself rightly understood by its friends and by those upon whom it showered its benefactions. The American man is at once superficially boastful and profoundly shy; he will propose to the admiration of others some of the mechanical gadgets of his civilization, but he will be embarrassed to talk about the soul of his country, its idealism, its culture, its intellectual achievement. A feeling of embarrassment seizes him when American novels, paintings, or musical compositions are admired abroad. Foreigners who have settled in America and are in a position to judge the truly great achievements of American universities, of education, of research foundations, the unbounded promise offered today by the quality of American youth, have a role to play. They are best able, when they visit Europe or write for Europeans, to stress the elements of American culture which are often underrated abroad, and the true reasons why the rest of the world may well be induced to set its hope in the country without which the world cannot save itself; and the true reasons are the intellectual and spiritual forces which are at work in this country. Better than even the Palomar telescope, electron microscopes, and the Mayo Clinic, to which any European scientific visitor will readily pay homage, are the faith, the imagination, the devotion to man and to the future which made those possible. The foreign-born student of literature, who may be credited with wielding words and a pen more readily than the scientist or the man of affairs, has a duty to perform as interpreter of America to Europe. For with all the mass media of today and the loud propaganda techniques in use, America is a strangely misinterpreted country and its true qualities are often unacknowledged.

The pioneers who first developed this continent and the emigrants who followed them in the nineteenth century were predominantly artisans, workmen, and peasants from Europe. They found unlimited possibilities when they landed in the New World, but also unlimited hardships. They had to be obsessed by the practical and, since most of them were compatriots of Robinson Crusoe, their genius lay in the realm of the practical. The culture of the country therefore took on a line from which it has hardly swerved. Changing the world through technical applications of science or through education and religion tested by their pragmatic results has continued to be preferred to contemplation of the world, to speculation on the ultimate causes of phenomena, or to the sense of beauty. The gain to this country and to mankind has proved immeasurable. It hardly behooves us, literary scholars migrated from Europe, to talk condescendingly of American achievements in the realm of the *praxis* and to affect a false superiority because we read Plato and Hegel and delight in all that is apparently useless, from metaphysics to poetry. The know-how may be an overrated and over-used formula, but without it Europe would not have been saved in World War II, and today its culture might well have been engulfed by Russia.

But one thing strikes and haunts an admiring observer of this country, especially of the youth of this country: the lack of true and deep happiness in many Americans, the inordinate number of frustrations and inhibitions, of nervous defects manifested by stuttering and trembling, the frequent recourse, in the upper classes, to drinking as a means of forgetfulness or of escape, the fear of worry, of unbalance, of inadaptation in a large group of young Americans, and even of others who have ceased to be young but have not acquired serenity and inward peace. Let us grant that observers from Latin countries have a tendency to believe that they alone possess the secrets of sanity and of a happy sex life and are prone to boasting of what is left to them since other material advantages are denied them. Let us make an allowance for the sly pleasure which a foreigner tends to experience in declaring the nationals of another country universally crazy. And let us not forget that the progress of medicine in America has aimed largely at diagnosing evils which elsewhere did not receive a name and therefore remained ignored, and at pointing to the mental and psychosomatic sources of many of our troubles, as most of the germ diseases were being eradicated.

It remains nevertheless that many of us who have the future of America at heart cannot help being concerned by our observation of growing numbers of persons who seem to live on the verge or in the fear of disintegration. Breakdowns, failures of nerve, panicky terrors at themselves, psychiatric ills are all too frequent an occurrence in a land where the material level of existence has been raised higher than ever before in history and where happiness is supposed to be the goal of many. This writer for one has often been reminded, in observing his American friends and students, of John Stuart Mill's *Autobiography* and of the crisis undergone by the British philosopher whose early development had been too exclusively intellectual and had overlooked emotional forces, poetry, and beauty. The gospel of work and the philosophy of utilitarianism proved baneful to him, and analysis driven to an excess of dryness had worn away the capacity to feel. Coleridge's lines,

> Work without hope draws nectar in a sieve,
> And hope without an object cannot live,

he was to recite to himself after he had discovered Wordsworth and Coleridge and the love for poetry, which were to save him from his acute depression. We profoundly believe that the therapeutic virtue of poetry, of literature in general, of the arts has been underestimated in American education, and that "the study of literature," as our title puts it, should also be the enjoyment of literature.

We have lost much through neglecting one of the most beautiful words, and things, in the world, if rightly conceived: pleasure. Criticism, in the last decades, in its effort to ape science and to evolve a vocabulary similar to that of science, has been guilty. The teaching of literature has become more abstruse than any laboratory science. The sole concern seems to be for epistemological values, and a self-respecting sophomore scribbling an essay on Donne or Proust will use the word at least three times per page. Naïveté and naturalness are hunted out. No one is supposed to understand modern novels if he has not delved into symbols, into Jung's archetypes and ancestral myths, into Frazer and Jessie Weston, into Kenneth Burke and I. A. Richards. Our debt is certainly considerable to those great minds. But a businessman taking a daily train to his bank, a diplomat sailing to Europe, a scientist, or an intelligent lady no longer dares open a novel of some intellectual standing or a volume of critical essays for fear of being an intruder in a chapel where only an unhappy few may worship. We have systematically narrowed literature down through reducing it to "literature as such," and we no longer deserve the tribute paid to it by men of the past who advocated it for what it should be: refined pleasure.[1]

If a French-born writer, whose country has long been credited with some experience in the field of criticism, may presume to proffer some advice, he would suggest that, with the immense development of literary study in universities since 1920, American scholars and critics have not yet adequately discharged their duty to the writers and to the public. "Criticism stands like an interpreter between the inspired and the uninspired," said Carlyle. If the inspired are the creators themselves, they have scant reason for being grateful to critics. Except for some reviewers whose task is one of information and who, hurried by the journalistic mores of a country in which "news" is only what has just happened or what is going to appear the next day, critics seldom take the trouble to write a thoughtful appreciation of contemporary writers. Hart Crane had been in his watery grave for a decade or two when comprehensive studies of his poetry appeared. There are very few if any which evaluate Wallace Stevens, Robinson Jeffers, or E. E. Cummings as poets. Faulkner finally gained recognition because Europe had acclaimed him in earnest and the Nobel Prize consecrated his world fame. Even such accepted classics as Dos Passos and O'Neill have had very few worth-while critical appraisals devoted to their work.

---

[1] The scientist, Thomas H. Huxley, addressing the South London working men's college in 1868, reserved a large place for literature in his address: "A liberal education and where to find it." "For literature," he said, "is the greatest of all sources of refined pleasure, and one of the great uses of a liberal education is to enable us to enjoy that pleasure." Enjoyment has similarly disappeared from much of our criticism as it has from some of our abstract art and functional decoration, as we were yielding to a new wave of puritanism in disguise. Of too few of the critics writing today in America could it be said, as T. S. Eliot said of W. P. Ker: "He was always aware that the end of scholarship is understanding, and that the end of understanding poetry is enjoyment, and that this enjoyment is gusto disciplined by taste."

The result has been the intensification of the great cultural evil of American society: the isolation of the writer and of the artist, both rejected into a pessimism never equaled in any literature except perhaps that of Russia, driven to bitter hostility to all that stands for "the American way of life." The talent displayed since 1910 or 1919 by the men and women writers of America is second to none. But the literature of Hemingway, of Caldwell, 'of Steinbeck, and of minor luminaries like Saroyan and Capote, and that of Mailer and of James Jones hopelessly lacks two characteristics of a truly great literature: sympathy for the country that it portrays and a powerful intellectual and psychological content. Deriding Babbitt and salesmen and commuters, and singing the praise of some amusing outlaws of *Cannery Row* or of *Tortilla Flat,* of bullfighters or of huntsmen among the hills of Africa or of warriors rapturously basking in the love of Spanish or Italian ladies is entertaining for a while. But if American literature is to compete in solidity with the best that the French or the Russians have produced, it must also treat its characters with more seriousness, identify itself with average Americans and not only with primitives and violent outlaws, as Flaubert, Tolstoy, Proust did with their characters even while satirizing them. The lack of intellectual content and of a serious and constructive *Weltanschauung* has prevented a great age of American letters from ranking with the classics and claiming its share in the training of the young. Scholars and critics should have helped writers assume such a natural role.

On the other hand, we must confess that while appreciation of music and of painting has grown immensely in America in the last thirty years, qualitatively and quantitatively, the appreciation of literature has not increased in a manner commensurate with the extension of literacy and with the inordinate growth of the people who have gone to college. There lies the chief failure of educators and scholars. The number of magazines in which some pretense of interest in literature is retained has consistently decreased since *The Dial,* the *Bookman,* the *North American Review,* and several others were decently buried. The others have steadily and niggardly reduced the space given to critical essays. The American theatre is in a woeful plight, and very few thoughtful articles ever appear in which this plight is analyzed and remedies are proposed. Over two million young people attend college at present, and only a trickle of those ever continue reading serious books after they have entered "mature" life. Financial resources flow generously to those who undertake surveys of average communities in Middletown or Elmtown, studies of Russian, Chinese, or Indonesian behavior; they will soon implement Point Four, provide funds for other countries intent on spreading their own culture inside and outside their borders. But those same so-called research organizations are reluctant to assist literary magazines in America, the publication of critical and scholarly volumes; in a word, the diffusion of literary culture in the wealthiest but also perhaps the most incurious of great countries.

To many of the European intellectuals who have migrated to the United States and have insisted that the rest of the world is today appealing to America for more than technical know-how and material help, for an ideal and for an intellectual and imaginative crusade for a better world, such a failure on the part of American civilization to spread its literary culture without diluting its essential virtue is the one black spot on the horizon. A naturalized scholar and critic is thus led to the conviction that, while adding to the mass of extant knowledge is his own dearest pursuit, he must in this country bend more of his energy to win larger groups to the appreciation of cultural values and of other civilizations. He must become a popularizer in the good sense of the word and, as the French say, work at the democratic "diffusion" of knowledge and of artistic value even harder than at the acquisition and selfish enjoyment of it. In thinking and doing thus, he is not importing "foreign" and "arty" prejudices from Europe into the New World. He is confident that he is pursuing the true cultural development of America as it was envisioned by the great men who in the eighteenth century founded this country. He is faithful to the ideal set forth by two great Americans of the last century, whose words should conclude this essay. Oliver Wendell Holmes, warning us against the excessive stress on technical and specialized training in America, once wrote:

If a man is a specialist, it is most desirable that he should also be civilized . . . that he should see things in their proportion. Nay, more, that he should be passionate as well as reasonable, that he should be able not only to explain, but to feel; that the ardors of intellectual pursuit should be relieved by the charm of art, should be succeeded by the joy of life become an end in itself.

Walt Whitman, than whom no man spoke more nobly of literature, did not mince words when, soon after 1870, he asserted in a text published in *Democratic Vistas* that "our New World democracy, however great a success in uplifting the masses out of their sloughs, in materialistic developments . . . is an almost complete failure . . . in really grand religious, moral, literary and esthetic results." He counted on literature to achieve the redemption of woman and to voice the profoundest aspirations of America to the rest of the world:

Literature, in our day and for current purposes, is not only more eligible than all the other arts put together, but has become the only general means of morally influencing the world.

The History of Art

ERWIN PANOFSKY

Even when dealing with the remote past, the historian cannot be entirely objective. And in an account of his own experiences and reactions the personal factor becomes so important that it has to be extrapolated by a deliberate effort on the part of the reader. I must, therefore, begin with a few autobiographical data, difficult though it is to speak about oneself without conveying the impression of either false modesty or genuine conceit.

I first came to this country in the fall of 1931 upon the invitation of New York University. I was then professor of the history of art at Hamburg; and since this Hanseatic city was always proud of its cosmopolitan tradition, the authorities were not only glad to grant me a leave of absence for one semester but subsequently consented to an arrangement whereby I was permitted to spend alternate terms in Hamburg and New York. Thus for three successive years I commuted, as it were, across the Atlantic. And when the Nazis ousted all Jewish officials in the spring of 1933, I happened to be in New York while my family were still at home. I fondly remember the receipt of a long cable in German, informing me of my dismissal but sealed with a strip of green paper which bore the inscription: "Cordial Easter Greetings, Western Union."

These greetings proved to be a good omen. I returned to Hamburg only in order to wind up my private affairs and to attend to the Ph.D. examinations of a few loyal

82 ·

students (which, curiously enough, was possible in the
initial stages of the Nazi regime); and thanks to the self-
less efforts of my American friends and colleagues, unfor-
gettable and unforgotten, we could establish ourselves at
Princeton as early as 1934. For one year I held concurrent
lectureships at New York and Princeton universities, and
in 1935 I was invited to join the newly constituted humanistic faculty of the Institute for Advanced Study which
owes its reputation to the fact that its members do their
research work openly and their teaching surreptitiously,
whereas the opposite is true of so many other institutions
of learning. I, too, have thus continued to teach in various
places, with special regularity in Princeton and New York.

I am telling all this in order to make it perfectly clear
that my experiences in this country are somewhat atypical
in regard to both opportunities and limitations. As to the
opportunities: in contrast to nearly all my colleagues, including the American-born, I was never hampered by
excessive teaching obligations and never suffered from a
lack of research facilities; in contrast to so many immigrant scholars, I had the good fortune of coming to the
United States as a guest rather than a refugee; and, be it
said with deepest gratitude, no one has ever made me feel
the difference when my status suddenly changed in 1933.
As to the limitations: I neither know the South beyond
Asheville, N. C., nor the West beyond Chicago; and, much
to my regret, have never been for any length of time in
professional contact with undergraduate students.

I

Though rooted in a tradition that can be traced back
to the Italian Renaissance and, beyond that, to classical
antiquity, the history of art—that is to say, the historical
analysis and interpretation of man-made objects to which
we assign a more than utilitarian value, as opposed to

esthetics, criticism, connoisseurship and "appreciation" on the one hand, and to purely antiquarian studies on the other—is a comparatively recent addition to the family of academic disciplines. And it so happens that, as an American scholar expressed it, "its native tongue is German." It was in the German-speaking countries that it was first recognized as a full-fledged *Fach,* that it was cultivated with particular intensity, and that it exerted an increasingly noticeable influence upon adjacent fields, including even its elder and more conservative sister, classical archaeology. The first book to flaunt the phrase "history of art" on its title page was Winckelmann's *Geschichte der Kunst des Altertums* of 1764, and the methodical foundations of the new discipline were laid in Karl Friedrich von Rumohr's *Italienische Forschungen* of 1827. A full professorship was established at an even earlier date, 1813, at Göttingen, its first incumbent being the excellent Johann Dominic Fiorillo (in spite of his name a native of Hamburg). And in the course of the years the rapidly multiplying university chairs in Germany, Austria, and Switzerland were graced by men whose names have never lost their magic: Jakob Burckhardt, Julius von Schlosser, Franz Wickhoff, Alois Riegl, Max Dvořák, Georg Dehio, Heinrich Wölfflin, Aby Warburg, Adolph Goldschmidt, Wilhelm Vöge. It was also characteristic that the major public collections were directed by men no less prominent as scholars than as administrators and experts, from Adam Bartsch and Johann David Passavant to Wilhelm Bode, Friedrich Lippmann, Max J. Friedländer, and Georg Swarzenski.

In emphasizing these facts I feel myself free from what may be suspected as retroactive German patriotism. I am aware of the dangers inherent in what has been decried as "Teutonic" methods in the history of art and of the fact that the results of the early, perhaps too early, institutionalization of the discipline were not always desirable. I am convinced that every page by Léopold Delisle and Paul Durrieu, Louis Courajod and the Goncourt brothers, Montague Rhodes James (who wanted to be known as an "antiquarian") and Campbell Dodgson, Cornelis Hofstede de Groot and Georges Hulin de Loo outweighs a ton of German doctoral theses. And I can understand that from the point of view of an English gentleman the art historian is apt to look like a fellow who compares and analyzes the charms of his feminine acquaintances in public instead of making love to them in private or writing up their family trees*; even now no permanent art historical chairs exist at either Oxford or Cambridge. But the fact remains that at the time of the Great Exodus in the 1930's the German-speaking countries still held the leading position in the history of art—except for the United States of America.

II

Here the history of art had recapitulated within a few decades the development from Bellori and Baldinucci to Riegl and Goldschmidt much as the collecting activities of J. P. Morgan—beginning with small objects of enormous value in terms of material or working hours, and ending up with old-master drawings—had recapitulated the development from the Duc de Berry to Mariette and Croizat. Originally the private hobby of such men of affairs and letters as Henry Adams and Charles Eliot Norton (whose

* As kindly brought to my attention by a former student residing at Oxford for the time being, it was just about eight months after this lecture had been delivered at the University of Pennsylvania that the British Broadcasting Company carried two speeches in defense of the history of art: N. Pevsner, "Reflections on Not Teaching Art History" (*The Listener,* XLVIII, 1952, No. 1235, October 30, page 715 ff.); and E. Waterhouse, "Art as a Piece of History" (*ibidem,* No. 1236, November 6, page 761 ff.). These speeches, both very informative and the second extremely witty, were broadcast under the heading: "An Un-English Activity?"

Harvard lectures were described by his son as "Lectures on modern morals illustrated by the arts of the ancients"), art history evolved into an autonomous discipline from the beginning of the twentieth century, and after the First World War (which *terminus post quem* is, of course, of portentous significance) it began to challenge the supremacy, not only of the German-speaking countries, but of Europe as a whole. This was possible, not in spite but because of the fact that its founding fathers—such men as Allan Marquand, Charles Rufus Morey, Frank J. Mather, A. Kingsley Porter, Howard C. Butler, Paul J. Sachs—were not the products of an established tradition but had come to the history of art from classical philology, theology and philosophy, literature, architecture, or just collecting. They established a profession by following a vocation.

At the beginning, the new discipline had to fight its way out of an entanglement with practical art instruction, art appreciation, and that amorphous monster "general education." The early issues of the *Art Bulletin,* founded in 1913 and now recognized as the leading art historical periodical of the world, were chiefly devoted to such topics as "What Instruction in Art Should the College A.B. Course Offer to the Future Layman?"; "The Value of Art in a College Course"; "What People Enjoy in Pictures"; or "Preparation of the Child for a College Course in Art." Art history, as we know it, sneaked in by the back door, under the guise of classical archaeology ("The Meleager in the Fogg Museum and Related Works in America"), evaluation of contemporary phenomena ("The Art of Auguste Rodin") and, characteristically, book reviews. It was not until 1919 (one year after the armistice) that it was permitted to lift its ugly little head in large print. But in 1923, when the *Art Bulletin* carried ten unashamedly art historical articles and only one on art appreciation, and when it was found necessary to launch a competing periodical, the short-lived *Art Studies,* the battle was won (though occasional skirmishes may occur even now). And it was about this time that the European scholars, only a handful of whom had crossed the Atlantic thus far, began to sit up and take notice.

They knew, of course, that magnificent collections of all kinds had been formed in the United States and that several very good art historical books—to mention only Allan Marquand's numerous studies on the Della Robbia family (1912-1922), Frederick Mortimer Clapp's two books on Pontormo (1914 and 1916), E. Baldwin Smith's monograph on Early Christian ivories in Provence (1918)—had been written in America. They also had heard rumors to the effect that remarkable studies of a technical nature were going on in several American museums and at a university called Harvard; that a wealthy lady in New York had founded a reference library containing thousands and thousands of photographs; and that, from as early as 1917, another university, named Princeton, was building up a comprehensive Index of Christian Iconography. This was partly taken for granted and partly considered peculiar. But in 1923 and 1924 there appeared, nearly simultaneously, A. Kingsley Porter's *Romanesque Sculpture of the Pilgrimage Roads,* which with one fell swoop revolutionized the accepted ideas as to the chronology and diffusion of twelfth-century sculpture on the entire European continent; Albert M. Friend's famous essay proposing to locate one of the most important and enigmatical Carolingian schools in the Royal Abbey of Saint-Denis; and Charles Rufus Morey's "Sources of Mediaeval Style," which dared reduce the complexity of medieval art to three great currents much as Johannes Kepler had reduced the complexity of the solar system to three great laws. No European scholar—least of all the Germans and Austrians who, whatever may be said against them, were less afraid of foreign

literature than most Italians and nearly all Frenchmen—
could remain blind to the fact that the United States had
emerged as a major power in the·history of art; and that,
conversely, the history of art had assumed a new, distinc-
tive physiognomy in the United States.

The following decade—from 1923 to 1933—saw what in
retrospect will look like a Golden Age. Princeton, apart
from excavating in Asia Minor as well as in France, and
launching a great program of manuscript publication,
cemented a lasting tradition of fastidious scholarship in
Early Christian, Byzantine, and medieval art. Harvard
trained a multitude of enthusiastic and sophisticated young
men who manned an ever-growing number of ever-
expanding museums. Chandler R. Post and Walter W. S.
Cook established the long-neglected history of Spanish art
as a field in its own right. Fiske Kimball embarked upon
his epoch-making studies in the architecture and decoration of the Louis XIV, Régence, Louis XVI, and Rococo
styles. William M. Ivins opened up new vistas in the interpretation and evaluation of the graphic arts. Richard
Offner developed connoisseurship in the field of the Italian
Primitives into the closest possible approximation to an
exact science. A younger generation, now brilliantly represented by scholars such as Rensselaer Lee, Meyer Schapiro
and Millard Meiss, gave the first proofs of its remarkable
talents. The Museum of Modern Art, conceived by Alfred
Barr, began its meteoric rise. And it was at the height of these
developments that Hitler became the master of Germany.

III

In the New York of the early 1930's—especially if he
came early enough to witness the final phase of the prohibi-
tion era and found himself surrounded by an atmosphere
of cozy dissipation which is hard to describe and harder
to remember without a certain nostalgia—the European

art historian was at once bewildered, electrified, and elated. He feasted on the treasures assembled in museums, libraries, private collections, and dealers' galleries. He discovered that certain aspects of medieval painting and book illumination could be more exhaustively studied in this country than in Europe because, owing to a series of historical accidents, most of the pertinent material had found its way across the water. He was amazed that he could order a book at the New York Public Library without being introduced by an embassy or vouched for by two responsible citizens; that libraries were open in the evenings, some as long as until midnight; and that everybody seemed actually eager to make material accessible to him. Even the Museum of Modern Art, originally housed on the twelfth floor of the Heckscher Building and later moved to a modest old brownstone dwelling on its present site, permitted visitors to leave unsnubbed in those days. Librarians and curators seemed to consider themselves primarily as organs of transmission rather than "keepers" or *conservateurs*. Even more astonishing was the stupendous amount of activity in the art historian's world—activity not free from intellectual and social snobbery but always thoroughly stimulating: countless exhibitions and endless discussion; privately financed research projects, started today and abandoned tomorrow; lectures delivered not only in the seats of learning but also in the homes of the wealthy, the audience arriving in twelve-cylinder Cadillacs, seasoned Rolls-Royces, Pierce-Arrows, and Locomobiles. And beneath this glittering surface there could be felt the spirit of discovery and experimentation which, controlled by scholarly conscientiousness, lived in the work of the Kingsley Porters and the Charles Rufus Moreys.

Coming into its own after the First World War, American art history drew strength from what would have been a weakness twenty or thirty years before: from the cultural and geographical distance from Europe. It was, of course, important that the United States had emerged from the conflict as the only belligerent power with an unimpaired economy so that ample funds were available for travel, research facilities, and publication. But more consequential was the fact that the United States had come for the first time into active rather than passive contact with the Old World and kept up this contact in a spirit both of possessiveness and impartial observation.

Where the communications between the European countries, too close for speedy reconciliation and too poor for a speedy resumption of cultural exchange, remained disrupted for many years, the communications between Europe and the United States had been kept intact or were quickly restored. New York was a gigantic radio set capable of receiving and transmitting to a great number of stations which were unable to reach each other. But what made the greatest impression on the stranger when first becoming aware of what was happening in America was this: Where the European art historians were conditioned to think in terms of national and regional boundaries, no such limitations existed for the Americans.

The European scholars either unconsciously yielded to, or consciously struggled against, deep-rooted emotions which were traditionally attached to such questions as whether the cubiform capital was invented in Germany, France, or Italy, or whether the first rib-vaults were built in Milan, Morienval, Caën, or Durham; and the discussion of such questions tended to be confined to areas and periods on which attention had been focused for generations or at least decades. Seen from the other side of the Atlantic, the whole of Europe from Spain to the Eastern Mediterranean merged into one panorama the planes of which appeared at proper intervals and in equally sharp focus.

And as the American art historians were able to see the past in a perspective picture undistorted by national and regional bias, so were they able to see the present in a perspective picture undistorted by personal or institutional *parti pris.* In Europe—where all the significant "movements" in contemporary art, from French Impressionism to International Surrealism, from the Crystal Palace to the "Bauhaus," from the Morris Chair to the Aalto Chair, had come into being—there was, as a rule, no room for objective discussion, let alone historical analysis. The direct impact of the events forced the littérateurs into either defense or attack, and the more intelligent art historians into silence. In the United States such men as Alfred Barr and Henry-Russell Hitchcock, to name only two of the pioneers in this field, could look upon the contemporary scene with the same mixture of enthusiasm and detachment, and write about it with the same respect for historical method and concern for meticulous documentation, as are required of a study on fourteenth-century ivories or fifteenth-century prints. "Historical distance" (we normally require from sixty to eighty years) proved to be replaceable by cultural and geographical distance.

To be immediately and permanently exposed to an art history without provincial limitations in time and space, and to take part in the development of a discipline still animated by a spirit of youthful adventurousness, brought perhaps the most essential gains which the immigrant scholar could reap from his transmigration. But in addition it was a blessing for him to come into contact—and occasionally into conflict—with an Anglo-Saxon positivism which is, in principle, distrustful of abstract speculation; to become more acutely aware of the material problems (posed, for example, by the various techniques of painting and print-making and the static factors in architecture) which in Europe tended to be considered as the concern of museums and schools of technology rather than universities; and, last but not least, to be forced to express himself, for better or worse, in English.

In view of what has been said about the history of our discipline, it was inevitable that the vocabulary of art historical writing became more complex and elaborate in the German-speaking countries than anywhere else and finally developed into a technical language which—even before the Nazis made German literature unintelligible to uncontaminated Germans—was hard to penetrate. There are more words in our philosophy than are dreamt of in heaven and earth, and every German-educated art historian endeavoring to make himself understood in English had to make up his own dictionary. In doing so he realized that his native terminology was often either unnecessarily recondite or downright imprecise; the German language unfortunately permits a fairly trivial thought to declaim from behind a woolen curtain of apparent profundity and, conversely, a multitude of meanings to lurk behind one term. The word *taktisch,* for example, normally denoting "tactical" as opposed to "strategic," is used in art historical German as an equivalent of "tactile" or even "textural" as well as "tangible" or "palpable." And the ubiquitous adjective *malerisch* must be rendered, according to context, in seven or eight different ways: "picturesque" as in "picturesque disorder"; "pictorial" (or, rather horribly, "painterly") as opposed to "plastic"; "dissolved," "sfumato," or "non-linear" as opposed to "linear" or "clearly defined"; "loose" as opposed to "tight"; "impasto" as opposed to "smooth." In short, when speaking or writing English, even an art historian must more or less know what he means and mean what he says, and this compulsion was exceedingly wholesome for all of us. Indeed this very compulsion, combined with the fact that the American professor is much more frequently called upon to face a nonprofessional and unfamiliar audience than is his European confrère, went a long way to loosen our tongues, if I may say so. Forced to express ourselves both understandably and precisely, and realizing, not without surprise, that it could be done, we suddenly found the courage to write books on whole masters or whole periods instead of—or besides—writing a dozen specialized articles; and dared to deal with, say, the problem of classical mythology in medieval art in its entirety instead of—or besides—investigating only the transformations of Hercules or Venus.

These, then, are some of the spiritual blessings which this country has bestowed upon the immigrant art historians. Whether and in what way they may have been able to reciprocate is not for me to say. But I should like to mention that, from a purely temporal point of view, their influx has unquestionably contributed to the further growth of the history of art as an academic discipline as well as an object of public interest. No foreign art historian has, to the best of my knowledge, ever displaced an American-born. The immigrants were either added to the staffs of college or university departments already in being (museums were, for understandable but somewhat delicate reasons, not equally eager to welcome them), or were entrusted with the task of instituting the teaching of the history of art where it had previously been absent from the scene. In either case the opportunities of American students and teachers were widened rather than narrowed. And in one case a group of refugee scholars has been privileged to play a constructive role in a development that may well be called spectacular: the rise of the Institute of Fine Arts of New York University.

It grew out of the small graduate department which it was my good fortune to join in 1931, and which, at that time, had about a dozen students, three or four professors, no rooms, let alone a building, of its own, and no equipment whatsoever. Both lecture and seminar courses were held in the basement rooms of the Metropolitan Museum, commonly referred to as "the funeral parlors," where smoking was forbidden under penalty of death and stern-faced attendants would turn us out at 8:55 P.M., regardless of how far the report or discussion had proceeded. The only thing to do was to adjourn to a nice speakeasy on Fifty-second Street; and this arrangement, laying the basis for several lasting friendships, worked very well for a term or two. But the days of speakeasies were numbered, and it was felt that the students of a big-town university needed a place, however small, where they might meet, smoke, and talk about their work during the day, without either drinks or professorial supervision, and in closer proximity to the Metropolitan Museum. Thus a tiny apartment was rented on the corner of Eighty-third Street and Madison Avenue, housing such lantern slides as had been accumulated by the individual lecturers and one of those standard sets of art books which could be obtained, upon request, from the Carnegie Corporation.

In the course of the next few years no less than five distinguished German refugees were called to permanent positions at what had now become the Institute of Fine Arts. Considerable funds were raised in mysterious fashion. And today this Institute, so far as I know the only independent university organ exclusively devoted to graduate instruction in the history of art, is not only the largest but also the most animated and versatile school of its kind, occupying a six-story building on East Eightieth Street, owning a workable library and one of the best collections of lantern slides, attended by well over a hundred graduate students advanced and enterprising enough to publish a scholarly periodical of their own, and counting among its alumni some of the most prominent academic teachers and museum men. All of which, however, would not have been possible had not the chairman, Walter Cook, shown an unparalleled combination of foresight, doggedness, business sense, self-effacing devotion, and lack of prejudice ("Hitler is my best friend," he used to say; "he shakes the tree and I collect the apples"), and had he not been given his chance by the providential synchronism between the rise of Fascism and Nazism in Europe and the spontaneous efflorescence of the history of art in the United States.

IV

I have just mentioned that the American scholar more frequently faces a nonprofessional and unfamiliar audience than does the European. On the one hand, this can be explained by general considerations. For reasons insufficiently explored by anthropologists, Americans seem to be genuinely fond of listening to lectures (a fondness encouraged and exploited by our museums which, unlike most of their sister institutions in Europe, think of themselves as cultural centers rather than as mere collections), and of attending conferences and symposia. And the "ivory tower" in which a professor is supposed to spend his life— a figure of speech, by the way, which owes its existence to a nineteenth-century conflation of a simile from the *Song of Songs* and Danaë's tower in Horace—has many more windows in the comparatively fluid society of this country than in most others. On the other hand, the larger radius of professorial activities results, to some extent, from the specific conditions of academic life in America. And this brings me to a brief discussion of what may be called organizational questions—a discussion which will somewhat transcend my subject because what applies to the history of art applies, *mutatis mutandis,* to all other branches of the humanities.

One basic difference between academic life in the

United States and Germany (I wish to limit myself to firsthand experience)[1] is that in Germany the professors are stationary and the students mobile, whereas the opposite is true in the United States. A German professor either remains in Tübingen until he dies, or he is called to Heidelberg and then, perhaps, to Munich or Berlin; but wherever he stays he stays put. It is part of his duties to give at stated intervals, in addition to specialized lecture courses and seminars, a so-called *collegium publicum*,[2] that is to say, a series of weekly lectures dealing with a subject of more general interest, free of charge and open to all students, faculty members, and, as a rule, the general public; but he rarely ascends a platform outside his perma-

[1] My comments on the organization of German universities (largely identical with that of the universities in Austria and Switzerland) refer, of course, to the period before Hitler whose regime destroyed the very foundations of academic life in Germany and Austria. With some reservations, however, they would seem to be valid also for the period after 1945 when, so far as I know, the *status quo* was more or less restored; such minor changes as have come to my notice are mentioned in notes 2 and 4. For further information, see the fundamental work by A. Flexner, *Universities, American, English, German* (New York, London, Toronto, 1930); and the entertaining account in E. H. Kantorowicz, "How the Pre-Hitler German Universities Were Run," *Western College Association; Addresses on the Problem of Administrative Overhead and the Harvard Report: General Education in a Free Society,* Fall Meeting, November 10, 1945, Mills College, Cal., pp. 3 ff.

[2] Specialized lecture courses are given *privatim*, that is to say, the students have to register for them and pay a moderate fee (about 60 cents) per weekly hour for each semester. Seminars, on the other hand, used to be given *privatissime et gratis*, that is to say, the students did not pay any fee while the instructor, and he alone, had the right to accept the participants according to his requirements. Now, I learn, seminars (except for the most advanced ones, given for the special benefit of candidates for the Ph.D.) are subject to the same fee as the *privatim* lecture courses; but the instructor still enjoys the right of admission. In addition to the fees for individual courses, of which he must take a minimum number while their choice is his own affair, the German student of a humanistic discipline pays only a registration fee for each term, plus an "admission fee" which includes permission to use the library and seminars as well as the right to medical service, etc.

nent habitat, except for professional meetings or congresses. The German student, however, his *abiturium* (final diploma of a recognized secondary school) entitling him to enroll at whichever university he pleases, spends one semester here and another there until he has found a teacher under whose direction he wishes to prepare his doctoral thesis (there are no bachelors' and masters' degrees in German universities) and who accepts him, so to speak, as a personal pupil. He can study as long as he wishes, and even after having settled down for his doctorate he may periodically disappear for any length of time.

Here, as we all know, the situation is reversed. Our older colleges and universities, all private and thus dependent on that alumni loyalty which in this country is as powerful a force as public school loyalty is in England, reserve the right of admission and keep the undergraduates for four entire years. State institutions, though legally obliged to accept every accredited student from their state, maintain at least the principle of permanency. Transfers are looked upon with marked disapprobation. And even graduate students stay, if possible, in one and the same school until they acquire their master's degree. But, as if to make up, to some extent, for the ensuing sameness of environment and instruction, both colleges and universities freely invite guest lecturers and guest professors, now for one evening, now for some weeks, now for a term or even a year.

From the point of view of the visiting lecturer, this system has many advantages. It widens his horizon, brings him into contact with colleagues and students of greatly different types, and, after some years, may give him a delightful sense of being at home on many campuses much as the itinerant humanists of the Renaissance were at home in many cities or courts. But from the point of view of the student—the student, that is, who plans to take up humanistic scholarship as a profession—it has obvious drawbacks. More often than not he enters a given college because family tradition or financial reasons leave him no other choice, and a given graduate school because it happens to accept him. Even if he is satisfied with his choice the impracticability of exploring other possibilities will narrow his outlook and impair his initiative, and if he has made a mistake the situation may develop into a real tragedy. In this event, the temporary contact with visiting lecturers will hardly suffice to counterbalance the crippling effect of an unsuitable environment and may even sharpen the student's sense of frustration.

No sensible person would propose to change a system which has developed for good historical and economic reasons and could not be altered without a basic revision of American ideas and ideals. I merely want to point out that it has, like all man-made institutions, the defects of its qualities. And this also applies to other organizational features in which our academic life differs from that in Europe.

One of the most important of these differences is the division of our colleges and universities into autonomous departments, a system foreign to the European mind. In conformity with medieval tradition, the universities on the European continent in general, and those of the German-speaking countries in particular, are organized into four, or five "faculties": theology, law, medicine, and philosophy (the last-named frequently divided into mathematics and natural science as opposed to the humanities). In each of these faculties there is one chair—only exceptionally more than one—devoted to such special disciplines as, to limit the discussion to the humanities, Greek, Latin, English, Islamic Languages, Classical Archaeology, or, for that matter, the History of Art; and it is, in principle, exclusively of the incumbents of these chairs, normally

full professors *(ordinarii),* that the faculties are composed.³
The full professor forms the nucleus of a small group of
what, very roughly, corresponds to associate professors
(extraordinarii) and assistant professors *(Privatdozenten)*⁴

³ After the First World War the German *Privatdozenten* and *extraordinarii* (cf. following note) won the right to be represented on the faculty
by delegates who, of course, occupy their seats as representatives of their
group, and not of their discipline, and are elected for only one year; when
I was in Hamburg they even had to leave the room when matters pertain-
ing to their discipline were discussed. As to the *etatsmässige extraordinarii*
(cf. again the following note) the custom varies. In most universities they
have a seat on the faculty only if their discipline is not represented by
an *ordinarius.*

⁴ This correspondence is indeed a *very* rough one. On the one hand,
the academic status of a *Privatdozent* (our "instructor" has no equivalent
in German universities) was and is more assured and dignified than that of
even our associate professors without tenure in that he enjoys perfect freedom of teaching and is as irremovable from office as the full professor.
On the other hand, this office carries, as its name implies, no remuneration
(until quite recently in certain universities). Having been granted the
venia legendi (permission to teach) on the basis of his scholastic merits
(documented by a *Habilitationsschrift* and a paper read to the faculty)
rather than having been "hired" to fill a gap in the curriculum, the
Privatdozent can claim only the fees paid by the students for his *privatim*
lecture courses and seminars (cf. note 2). He receives a fixed salary only
if he either obtains a *Lehrauftrag* (commission to teach) in a specified
subject or accepts an assistantship, in which case he shoulders a goodly
part of the work involved in the administration of the seminar or institute.
Otherwise he depends on outside income or such subventions as may be
obtained from official or semiofficial foundations. The somewhat paradoxi-
cal nature of this arrangement became especially apparent during the
difficult period after the First World War and may be illustrated by my
personal experience. I had become (upon invitation) a *Privatdozent* at
Hamburg University, founded as late as 1920, in 1921; and since I was
the only "full-time" representative of my discipline (other lectures and
seminars being given by the directors and curators of the local museums),
I was entrusted with the directorship of the nascent art historical seminar
and had the unusual privilege of accepting and examining candidates for
the doctorate. I received, however, no salary; and when, by 1923, my
private fortune had been consumed by the inflation I was made a paid
assistant of the very seminar of which I was the unpaid director. This
interesting post of assistant to myself, created by a benevolent Senate
because the salary attached to an assistantship was somewhat higher than
a *Lehrauftrag,* I held until I was appointed full professor, skipping the
stage of *extraordinarius,* in 1926. Today, I learn, the *Privatdozenten* in
some West German universities receive a stipend *ex officio;* but this entails
a restriction of their previously illimited number, the extension of the

over whom he has, however, no formal authority as to their academic activities. He is responsible for the administration of his seminar or institute; but the awarding of degrees and the admission or invitation of teaching personnel, regardless of rank, is decided upon by the whole faculty.

To one accustomed to our system of self-governing departments operating directly under the deities this time-honored arrangement sounds rather absurd. When a candidate submits a doctoral thesis on the development of the diacritical signs in Arabic, the full professor of the history of art has a voice in the matter while the associate and assistant professors of Islamic Languages have not. No full professor, however unsuited for administrative work, can be relieved of his duty to conduct the affairs of his seminar or institute. No *Privatdozent,* however unsuccessful, can be discharged except by disciplinary action. He can neither be assigned a specific lecture or seminar course (unless he has accepted a special *Lehrauftrag* comparable to the contract of a "Visiting Lecturer" here), nor can he legally be prevented from giving any lecture or seminar course he pleases, regardless of the comfort of his full professor, as long as he keeps within the limitations of his *venia legendi* ("permission to teach").[5]

But here again the American system has the faults of its virtues (among the latter, incidentally, is a most healthy elasticity which permits, for example, older graduate stu-

---

minimum interval between doctorate and admission to a *Privatdozentur* from two years to three, and the introduction of an intermediary examination after which the candidate bears the beautiful title *Doctor habil* [*itandus*]. The *extraordinarii* fall into two very different classes. They are either older *Privatdozenten* to whom a professorial title has been given by courtesy and without any material change of status, or *etatsmässige* ("budgeted") *extraordinarii* whose position is similar to that of the full professors, except for the fact that their salaries are smaller and that they have, as a rule, no seat on the faculty (cf. preceding note).

[5] Cf. preceding note.

dents to do some teaching, either in their own university or in a neighboring institution). The American associate or assistant professor has a full vote at departmental meetings; but he must give the courses which the department assigns to him. The affairs of the French Department cannot be interfered with by even the fullest professor of modern history or *vice versa;* but just this perfect autonomy of the departments entails two grave dangers: isolation and inbreeding.

The art historian may know as little of the diacritical signs in Arabic as the Arabist does of Caravaggio. But that the two gentlemen are bound to see each other every fortnight at a faculty meeting is good for them because they may have, or develop, a common interest in Neo-Platonism or astrological illustrations; and it is good for the university because they may have well-founded, if divergent, views about general policies which may be profitably discussed *in pleno.* The professor of Greek may know nothing of Chaucer and Lydgate; but it is useful that he has the right to ask whether the professor of English, in proposing a nice young man for an associate professorship, may not have inadvertently overlooked some other young man perhaps less nice but possibly more capable. In fact, our institutions of learning are becoming more and more acutely aware of these two dangers, isolation and inbreeding. The University of Chicago has attempted to coördinate the humanistic departments into one "division"; other universities try interdepartmental committees and/or courses; Harvard goes so far as to make a permanent appointment in, say, the Department of Classics only after convoking an "*ad hoc* committee" composed of Harvard professors other than classicists and classicists from institutions other than Harvard. But to coördinate sovereign departments into a "division" is about as easy as to coördinate sovereign states into an international organization, and the appointment of committees may be said to indicate the presence of a problem rather than solve it.

V

Needless to say, this difference between the "departmental system" and the "chair system," as it may be called, reflects not only a divergence in political and economic conditions but also a divergence in the concept of "higher education" as such. Ideally (and I know full well that the European ideal has undergone, and is still undergoing, no less significant a change than the American reality), the European university, *universitas magistrorum et scholarium,* is a body of scholars, each surrounded by a cluster of *famuli.* The American college is a body of students entrusted to a teaching staff. The European student, unsupervised except for such assistance and criticism as he receives in seminars and personal conversation, is expected to learn what he wants and can, the responsibility for failure or success resting exclusively with himself. The American student, tested and graded without cease, is expected to learn what he must, the responsibility for failure or success resting largely with his instructors (hence the recurrent discussions in our campus papers as to how seriously the members of the teaching staff violate their duties when spending time on research). And the most basic problem which I have observed or encountered in our academic life is how to achieve an organic transition from the attitude of the student who feels: "You are paid for educating me; now, damn you, educate me," to that of the young scholar who feels: "You are supposed to know how to solve a problem; now, please, show me how to do it"; and, on the part of the instructor, from the attitude of the taskmaster who devises and grades test papers producing the officially required percentage of failures, passes, and honors, to that of the gardener who tries to make a tree grow.

This transformation is presumed to take place in the graduate school and to reach perfection in the following years. But the sad fact is that the average graduate student (a really superior talent will assert itself in the face of any system) finds himself in a position which makes it more difficult for him to achieve intellectual independence than for a certain group of undergraduates—those, that is, who, owing to their high scholastic standing, are freed from compulsory classes during their senior year.

It is the chairman of the department who assigns to the graduate student a number of courses and seminars each term (and far too many in most cases), in which he has to struggle for high marks. The subject of his master's thesis is, more often than not, determined by one of his instructors who also supervises its progress. And at the end he faces an examination, concocted by the whole department, which no single member thereof could pass in creditable fashion.

There is, by and large, any amount of good will on both sides; kindliness and helpful solicitude on the part of the teacher and—I speak from happiest experience—loyalty and responsiveness on the part of the student. But within the framework of our system just these engaging qualities seem to make the transformation from student into scholar so much the harder. Most graduate students in the humanities are not financially independent. In a society which, for good and sufficient reasons, rates the scholar considerably below the lawyer, the doctor, and, quite particularly, the successful businessman, it takes a strong will and something akin to obsession for the scion of a wealthy family to break down the resistance of his parents, uncles, and club friends when he proposes to follow a calling the highest possible reward of which is a professorship with eight or ten thousand dollars a year. The average graduate student, therefore, does not come from a wealthy family and must try to prepare himself for a job as fast as he can, and this in such a way that he is able to accept whatever offers. If he is an art historian, he expects his teachers to endow him with the ability either to enter any department of any museum or to give any course in any college; and the teachers do their best to live up to this expectation. As a result, graduate student and graduate teacher alike are haunted by what I should like to call the specter of completeness.

In German universities this specter of completeness—or, to be more polite, the preoccupation with the "balanced curriculum"—does not exist. In the first place, the freedom of movement enjoyed by the students makes completeness unnecessary. The professors lecture on whichever subject fascinates them at the time, thereby sharing with their students the pleasures of discovery; and if a young man happens to be interested in a special field in which no courses are available at one university, he can, and will, go to another. In the second place, the aim of the academic process as such is to impart to the student, not a maximum of knowledge but a maximum of adaptability—not so much to teach him subject matter as to teach him method. When the art historian leaves the university his most valuable possession is neither the fairly uneven acquaintance with the general development of art which he is expected to acquire through lecture courses, seminars, and private reading, nor the more thorough familiarity with the special field from which the subject of his thesis has been taken, but an ability to turn himself into a specialist in whichever domain may happen to attract his fancy in later life. As time goes on, the world of the German art historian —and this writer is no exception—tends to resemble an archipelago of little islands forming, perhaps, a coherent pattern when viewed from an airplane but separated by channels of abysmal ignorance; whereas the world of his American confrère may be compared to a massive table-land of specialized knowledge overlooking a desert of general information.

After the final degree—and this is another important difference—the German art historian, provided he wishes to enter the academic career, is on his own for some time. He cannot be admitted to a teaching position before at least two or even three years have passed and he has produced a solid piece of work, the subject of which may or may not be connected with that of his doctoral thesis. And after having received the *venia legendi* he is, as mentioned earlier, at liberty to teach as much or as little as he sees fit. The young American master of arts or master of fine arts, however, will, as a rule, at once accept an instructorship or assistant professorship which normally entails a definite and often quite considerable number of teaching hours and in addition—owing to a recent development which I consider unfortunate—imposes upon him the tacit obligation to prepare himself, as speedily as possible, for a doctor's degree as a prerequisite of promotion. He still remains a cogwheel in a machinery, only that he now grades instead of being graded, and it is difficult for him to achieve that balance between teaching and research which is perhaps the finest thing in academic life.

Too often burdened with an excessive "teaching load"—a disgusting expression which in itself is a telling symptom of the malady I am trying to describe—and no less often cut off from the necessary facilities, the young instructor or assistant professor is rarely in a position to follow up the problems encountered in the preparation of his classes; so that both he and his students miss the joyful and instructive experience which comes from a common venture

into the unexplored. And never during his formative years
has he had a chance to fool around, so to speak. Yet it is
precisely this chance which makes the humanist. Humanists cannot be "trained"; they must be allowed to mature
or, if I may use so homely a simile, to marinate. It is not
the reading matter assigned for Course 301 but a line of
Erasmus of Rotterdam, or Spenser, or Dante, or some
obscure mythographer of the fourteenth century, which
will "light our candle"; and it is mostly where we have no
business to seek that we shall find. *Liber non est*, says a
delightful Latin proverb, *qui non aliquando nihil agit*:
"He is not free who does not do nothing once in a while."

In this respect, too, considerable efforts at improvement
have been made in recent years. Most art departments no
longer insist on absolute omniscience in their M.A.'s,
M.F.A.'s and even Ph.D.'s, but allow one or two "areas
of concentration." A breathing spell between the end of
graduate school and the beginning of a "career" is provided, in a number of cases, by the Fulbright Fellowships
(which are, however, limited to study abroad and are ad-
ministered, as far as the final decisions are concerned, by
a political rather than scholastic agency). The same Fulbright Fellowships are also open to scholars already in
harness, if I may say so, and these can furthermore obtain
a year or two of unimpeded research by winning such
awards as a Guggenheim Fellowship or a temporary mem-
bership with the Institute for Advanced Study which con-
siders this kind of service as one of its principal functions.
Grants of this type, of course, take the incumbent out of
teaching altogether. But even the problem of balance between teaching and research has, fortunately, begun to
attract some attention. A few universities, notably Yale,
make use of special funds to cut the teaching obligations
of promising young faculty members in half for a number
of years without reducing their salaries.

VI

Yet much remains to be done. And nothing short of a miracle can reach what I consider the root of our troubles, the lack of adequate preparation at the high school stage. Our public high schools—and even an increasing number of the fashionable and expensive private schools—dismiss the future humanist with deficiencies which in ,many cases can never be completely cured and can be relieved only at the expense of more time and energy than can reasonably be spared in college and graduate school. First of all, it is, I think, a mistake to force boys and girls to make a decision between different kinds of curricula, some of them including no classical language, others no mathematics to speak of, at an age when they cannot possibly know what they will need in later life. I have still to meet the humanist who regrets that he had to learn some mathematics and physics in his high school days. Conversely, Robert Bunsen, one of the greatest scientists in history, is on record with the statement that a boy who is taught nothing but mathematics will not become a mathematician but an ass, and that the most effective education of the youthful mind is a course in Latin grammar.[6]

However, even assuming that the future humanist was lucky enough to choose the right curriculum when he was thirteen or fourteen (and a recent survey has disclosed that of the million high school students in New York City only

[6] It may not be amiss to reprint in full Bunsen's statement, transmitted by an ear-witness who was a biologist: "Im Anschluss an Gauss kam Bunsen auf die Frage zu sprechen, in welcher Weise man einen für Mathematik besonders begabten Jungen erziehen solle. 'Wenn Sie ihm nur Mathematik beibringen, glauben Sie, dass er ein Mathematiker werden wird?—Nein, ein Esel.' Für besonders wichtig erklärte er die Denkerziehung durch die lateinische Grammatik. In ihr lernen die Kinder mit Gedankendingen umgehen, die sie nicht mit Händen greifen können, die jedoch einer Gesetzmässigkeit unterliegen. Nur so lernen sie es, mit Begriffen sicher umzugehen." Cf. J. von Uexküll, *Niegeschaute Welten; Die Umwelten meiner Freunde* (Berlin, 1936), p. 142.

one thousand take Latin and only fourteen Greek), even then he has, as a rule, not been exposed to that peculiar and elusive spirit of scholarship which Gilbert Murray calls *religio grammatici*—that queer religion which makes its votaries both restless and serene, enthusiastic and pedantic, scrupulously honest and not a little vain. The American theory of education requires that the teachers of the young—a vast majority of them females—know a great deal about "behavior patterns," "group integration," and "controlled aggression drives," but does not insist too much upon what they may know of their subject, and cares even less for whether they are genuinely interested or actively engaged in it. The typical German "Gymnasial-professor" is—or at least was in my time—a man of many shortcomings, now pompous, now shy, often neglectful of his appearance, and blissfully ignorant of juvenile psychology. But though he was content to teach boys rather than university students, he was nearly always a scholar. The man who taught me Latin was a friend of Theodor Mommsen and one of the most respected Cicero specialists. The man who taught me Greek was the editor of the *Berliner Philologische Wochenschrift,* and I shall never forget the impression which this lovable pedant made on us boys of fifteen when he apologized for having overlooked the misplacement of a comma in a Plato passage. "It was my error," he said, "and yet I have written an article on this very comma twenty years ago; now we must do the translation over again." Nor shall I forget his antipode, a man of Erasmian wit and erudition, who became our history teacher when we had reached the stage of "high school juniors" and introduced himself with the words: "Gentlemen, this year we shall try to understand what happened during the so-called Middle Ages. Facts will be presupposed; you are old enough to use books."

It is the sum total of little experiences like these which

makes for an education. This education should begin as early as possible, when minds are more retentive than ever after. And what is true of method is also true, I think, of subject matter. I do not believe that children and boys should be taught only that which they can fully understand. It is, on the contrary, the half-digested phrase, the half-placed proper name, the half-understood verse, remembered for sound and rhythm rather than meaning, which persists in the memory, captures the imagination, and suddenly emerges, thirty or forty years later, when one encounters a picture based on Ovid's *Fasti* or a print exhibiting a motif suggested by the *Iliad*—much as a saturated solution of hyposulphite suddenly crystallizes when stirred.

If one of our great foundations were seriously interested in doing something for the humanities it might establish, *experimenti causa,* a number of model high schools sufficiently endowed with money and prestige to attract teaching faculties of the same caliber as those of a good college or university, and students prepared to submit to a program of study which our progressive educators would consider exorbitant as well as unprofitable. But the chances of such a venture are admittedly slim.

Apart from the apparently unsolvable problem of secondary education, however, the immigrant humanist, looking back over the last twenty years, has no cause for discouragement. Traditions, rooted in the soil of one country and one continent, cannot and should not be transplanted. But they can cross-fertilize, and this cross-fertilization, one feels, has been initiated and is in progress.

There is only one point which it would be disingenuous not to touch upon, though it may seem indelicate to do so: the terrifying rise of precisely those forces which drove us out of Europe in the 1930's: nationalism and intolerance. We must, of course, be careful not to jump to conclusions. The foreigner is inclined to forget that history never repeats itself, at least not literally. The same virus produces different effects in different organisms, and one of the most hopeful differences is that, by and large, the American university teachers seem to wrestle against the powers of darkness instead of ministering to them; in at least one memorable instance they have even found the support of an alumni committee the voice of which cannot be ignored in the land.[7] But we cannot blind ourselves to the fact that Americans may now be legally punished, not for what they do or have done, but for what they say or have said, think or have thought. And though the means of punishment are not the same as those employed by the Inquisition, they are uncomfortably similar: economic instead of physical strangulation, and the pillory instead of the stake.

Once dissent is equated with heresy, the foundations of the apparently harmless and uncontroversial humanities are no less seriously threatened than those of the natural and social sciences. There is but one step from persecuting the biologist who holds unorthodox views of heredity or the economist who doubts the divine nature of the free enterprise system, to persecuting the museum director who exhibits pictures deviating from the standards of Congressman Dondero or the art historian who fails to pronounce the name of Rembrandt Peale with the same reverence as that of Rembrandt van Rijn. But there is more to it.

The academic teacher must have the confidence of his students. They must be sure that, in his professional capacity, he will not say anything which to the best of his belief he cannot answer for, nor leave anything unsaid which to the best of his belief he ought to say. A teacher who, as a private individual, has permitted himself to be

[7] See the report of the Yale Alumni Committee "On the Intellectual and Spiritual Welfare of the University, Its Students and Its Faculty," reprinted in full, e.g., in *Princeton Alumni Weekly*, LII, No. 18 (March 29, 1952), p. 3.

frightened into signing a statement repugnant to his moral sense and his intellect, or, even worse, into remaining silent where he knows he ought to have spoken, feels in his heart that he has forfeited the right to demand this confidence. He faces his students with a clouded conscience, and a man with a clouded conscience is like a man diseased. Let us listen to Sebastian Castellio, the brave theologian and humanist who broke with Calvin because he could not dissimulate; who for many years supported his wife and children as a common laborer rather than be disloyal to what he believed to be true; and who, by the force of his indignation, compelled posterity to remember what Calvin had done to Michael Servetus. "To force conscience," Castellio says, "is worse than cruelly to kill a man. For to deny one's convictions destroys the soul."[8]

8 R. H. Bainton, "Sebastian Castellio, Champion of Religious Liberty, 1515-1563," *Castellioniana; Quatre études sur Sebastien Castellion et l'idée de la tolérance* (Leiden, 1941), pp. 25 ff.

The Scientists from Europe and Their New Environment

Wolfgang Köhler

I have been invited to speak about the immigration of European scientists in general. Unfortunately, this is too big a task for me. I propose to make only a few remarks about developments which, twenty years ago, followed the immigration of outstanding men in natural science, and will then turn to an entirely different immigration, which occurred in psychology, and began much earlier.

The influence of the immigration in natural science was immediate, and obviously all to the good. Since both among the Europeans and their American colleagues standards of experimentation and reasoning were extremely high, no serious disputes could ever arise between the two parties. Actually, among the newcomers many were well known in this country long before they immigrated. Most American scientists will nevertheless admit that closer personal relations soon increased the rate at which new discoveries were now made.

The men from Europe had not been here for many years when a situation arose in which some could show their intellectual power in a most frightening application of physics to public affairs. It was a mathematical physicist from Germany who, in a letter written in the fall of 1939, called President Roosevelt's attention to discoveries in subatomic physics which had recently been made by investigators in various countries. According to the physicist, so powerful a weapon might be constructed on the basis of these discoveries that even the strongest explosives so far produced in munition factories would look obsolete in comparison. The United States did not want to remain behind a potential enemy with regard to any weapon which human ingenuity could build at the time, and so the Manhattan Project came step by step into existence. Several European scientists played a leading part in the actual construction of what is now called the atomic bomb. When the first of these terrific devices had just destroyed large parts of a Japanese city, both Mr. Truman and Mr. Churchill found it necessary to explain to the world what had happened, and why they had believed that it must happen. Ever since, we have lived in a new era of political and military thought, torn between the hope that, after this extraordinary demonstration of man's ability to destroy, nations simply must learn to live together in peace—and a suspicion that even this lesson might not have been enough.

It is my impression that, on the whole, both the Americans and the Europeans who participated in this work intensely dislike their own creation. They probably hope never to see it used again in an attack on people, least of all on civilians. Science has never made a greater impact on mankind than it did by this sinister product of collaboration between physicists from abroad and Americans. To my regret, the great revelations about the nature of the physicial world, which made the bomb possible, have left most of us pretty cold. That fascinating achievement of the human mind which we call physics is in this country adequately known only to small groups. But we tremble when thinking of the fearsome consequences which would follow if it should next be our turn.

In the meantime, collaboration between the men from

Europe and the American physicists has become so inti-
mate that their descent from different cultural stocks is
half forgotten when they work together, excepting that the
two parties may sometimes tease each other. Thus a European might make a friendly joke about the American
tendency to emphasize so-called know-how, for instance, in
building ever bigger and better cyclotrons; and an American might retaliate by asking how the Europeans manage
to build a new universe every few years in mere thought—
not to mention their articles about the new models, which
read like modern poetry, and are equally hard to understand.

There has also been an immigration of excellent biologists, and the work of some has clearly added new ways of
studying living systems to the methods previously familiar
in America. One of the most important advances in biology
has, however, been brought about by physicists, in fact
precisely by the work of those who constructed the atomic
bomb. The "piles" which are used for this purpose yield
not only the substances which explode in atomic bombs
but also less harmful materials. While the atoms of these
materials are chemically equivalent to ordinary atoms,
such as those of carbon or phosphorus, they differ from
their common relatives by being radioactive. This means
that they announce their presence by electrical disturb-
ances in their environment, which can readily be detected.
Now, until recently, physiologists had considerable difficulties in tracing the course of various chemical substances
within the organism. At present these difficulties are gradually being overcome, because when the new radioactive
atoms are substituted for their ordinary counterparts they
form the same chemical compounds as these and are, in
such compounds, transported to the same places. There is
no serious interference with normal processes within the

organism while, nevertheless, the distribution of important chemicals in these processes can now be followed by means of sensitive electrical devices. For this reason the new elements are called "tracers." A whole literature is rapidly growing up in biology and medicine which is exclusively concerned with the paths of radioactive atoms in the body. It stands to reason that not only the physiology of normal organic processes but also the study of certain diseases must greatly profit from this excellent method. Physicists from abroad and their American colleagues are likely to feel considerably relieved when realizing that, in the long run, far more human lives may be saved in this fashion than have so far been destroyed by bombs which came from the same piles.

In this instance, the physicists' contribution to biology was only a by-product of work which originally had another purpose. But in recent times some physicists have turned to biological investigations quite deliberately. This is a new development which some time ago began in Europe, and is now spreading in America mostly under the influence of physicists from abroad. In more than one direction, physics has now advanced so far that, within the boundaries of this science, further progress in the same directions is hardly possible. But it seems that one cannot stop a good physicist. When he reaches a boundary, he finds it natural to look beyond. If what he sees appears to him interesting, he will presently trespass, and begin work on the other side. Now, beyond physics lies biology. The result is that some of the best physicists and chemists are now investigating fundamental problems in this science. For instance, such men are now making great progress in the study of viruses. What could be more fascinating than the behavior of these curious agents, which can in certain respects be compared with that of living matter, while in others it is that of enormous molecules? Most probably, such studies will also prove to have important consequences in medicine. For we all know that several dangerous diseases originate when viruses rathér than germs invade the organism.

Another fundamental problem in biology which is now being studied by physicists and chemists from Europe is that of photosynthesis. Most plants have the gift of combining simple chemical substances into organic compounds with the help of light. Without photosynthesis, there would be no human beings. We cannot live without food, and our food consists of organic substances which are formed either in plants or in animals. In the former case, the substances in question derive from simpler organic compounds which owe their existence to photosynthesis. But this is the ultimate origin of our food also in the latter case. For, in the last analysis, animal life is possible only because so many animals eat plants, and thus assimilate chemical compounds, the first origin of which is photosynthesis. Obviously, when we eat parts of carnivorous animals, the original source of our food is still the same. Thus, photosynthesis occupies a key position in general biology. If, therefore, exact science could fully clarify this particular process, our understanding of life in terms of more general principles would be greatly advanced.

I will now turn to my own field, which is psychology. But let us distinguish. Much psychological wisdom may be found in Cervantes, in Shakespeare, and in the great novelists of the nineteenth century. Psychology in this sense, I must say with regret, has never played an important role in the psychology with which I shall now deal, the psychology which claims to be a science. The former must therefore be excluded from my report. For another reason, I cannot discuss a certain field in which a mixture of psychoanalysis and social psychology is now rife. Let me mention only two discoveries in this field. The education of Japanese boys is very strict; therefore the adult Japanese is aggressive, and starts wars. Or, Russian babies have to wear their diapers extremely tight; therefore Russian grown-ups are not nice to the people of other countries. What particular fashion in diapers, long since discarded, must we blame for the fact that the now grown-up discoverers of such causal connections never feel the slightest need of proving that their assertions are right? This need is so strongly felt in what we call science that the discoveries themselves must here be ignored. In the following, I will mainly deal with those parts of psychology in which a solid core of knowledge is gradually being established.

It would be quite misleading to say that American psychology has merely been influenced by an immigration from Europe. In this respect, developments in psychology have differed entirely from those in the natural sciences. For, sixty or seventy years ago, American psychology as a whole was virtually created by the immigration of men and ideas from Europe. Moreover, one European psychologist after another then came to this country, and somehow affected the ways of American psychology long before Mussolini and Hitler came to power. The arrival of a few more European psychologists in the thirties could therefore no longer have a decisive influence upon further developments. Under these circumstances, I cannot restrict my remarks to the post-Hitler period. I must look farther back, and must describe how psychology as a science was first imported, how America reacted at the time, and how she reacted again when more and more psychologists arrived from abroad. Technical matters I cannot, of course, explain here. Rather, what I have to say will be related to issues in which many are likely to be interested. For my main theme is the way in which particular trends in the history of American psychology have sprung from far more general convictions held by individuals or groups, both American and European.

When, late in the nineteenth century and early in the twentieth, the student population of America began to grow in the most extraordinary fashion, and young people heard for the first time about the achievements of science, the effect on some must have been almost intoxicating. But, if natural science could make such an impression, how utterly fascinating must have been the news that, just a short time ago, the Germans had succeeded in establishing a rigorous science also of the mind. Obviously the new discipline could best be studied at its source. Thus American psychology came into being when a number of young people first went to Germany to study experimental psychology under Wundt in Leipzig, and then returned to America, where they promptly founded psychological laboratories in the German style. As a result, early American psychology had an unmistakable European flavor. It also happened that presently a few Europeans came over, who were equally enthusiastic about the new science, who knew it even better, and among whom at least one, the Englishman Titchener, was not only an expert in Wundt's psychology but also a most powerful person. At the time, the Germans used two procedures: one consisted of experimentation and measurement, preferably in the fields of sensation and memory; in the other, simple human experiences were established in trained observers, and then critically inspected, until their true nature, no longer discolored by any impurities, was finally revealed. It was these procedures which Titchener and others recommended to their American students.

Neither one technique nor the other appealed to William James of Harvard. His eyes were open to anything that passes through human minds, and he had just gathered into a great treatise what he had found there. One can hardly say that his contempt for the new psychology was only an American reaction. Rather, it was the reaction of a man who felt life more strongly than most others, who was intensely interested in philosophical problems, and who had an unfailing sense of proportion. The new endeavor seemed to him unbelievably pretentious with its scientific trimmings, pathetically narrow in scope, and therefore boring almost beyond endurance. Why did the new psychologists measure at all, if what they measured were unimportant nuances of sensation and the like? He strongly felt that when people begin to measure for the sake of measuring, and thus to deal with small things which alone can be so treated, the existence of all greater things will eventually be ignored. While little harm would be done in this fashion if the mistake were made in some corner of natural science, results were bound to be deplorable when the subject matter in question was the most important of all, the nature of man himself. This part of the world, James felt, should not be so distorted under any circumstances, not even in the name of science. We remember that it was William James who once, embittered by the one-track mentality of certain scientists, ascribed to them the slogan: *Fiat scientia, pereat mundus*, which may loosely be translated as "Science comes first. If meanwhile the world goes to pieces, we do not care."

The new psychologists, on the other hand, paid little attention to William James. For, with his need for a wider visual field, he did not spend untold days in a laboratory; he refused to measure, because he was not interested in what was being measured; and the full drama of mental life remained to him incomparably more important than the fact that, in detail, something had now become possible in psychology that resembled science. Apparently he was not a scientist at all. To a degree, the contrast between James's view and that of the experimentalists-at-all-costs still exists, and it will not entirely disappear until scientific psychology has become great enough for its tremendous task.

I mentioned two procedures which were initially recommended in the new science: the various techniques of experimentation, and the patient observation of certain mental data as such. The latter procedure was not accepted for long in America. Impatient young Americans would soon ask: "Is the study of psychological events to be postponed until the last static element of human experience has been sufficiently inspected? Why not start at once with the investigation of what actually happens, that is, of mental function?" They had hardly spoken when much louder voices were raised which demanded that the second procedure, the inspection of mental data as such, be given up entirely. The voices were those of the early American behaviorists. "What is this," they would say, "a science, or one more version of old-fashioned philosophical speculation? We are invited to inspect what is happening in our own minds? As scientists, we strongly object to this advice. So-called mental facts do not constitute a material with which a real science can deal with any confidence. In science, one observes only what is accessible to everybody. No other observation can be called objective. But in the alleged inspection of mental data a person is concerned with purely subjective phenomena to which nobody but he has any access. To make things worse, no second person can ever be sure that in a first person there are any mental facts at all. Psychologists should therefore study only a subject's vocalizations, which are physical sounds, or the movements of his face, or those of other parts of his body. In other words, so long as psychological procedures claim to be scientific they must be restricted to the study of behavior."

I wonder whether the word "science" has ever been

written in bigger capitals than it was by the behaviorists. Epistemologically, of course, their argument was rather naïve. It could easily be turned upside down on the ground that no physicist, and also no behaviorist, can ever directly observe the objective facts of which the behaviorists were so fond. Such facts become known only by perception, that is, by one of the subjective phenomena with which the behaviorists did not want to deal. At the present time we no longer get excited about such errors. They go with being very young. It takes some time to become mature, and history seems to have no treatment by which the process can be greatly accelerated. Also, it is only fair to add that during the past forty years behaviorism has changed considerably; there is far more sophistication in its present attitude than could be discovered in its early statements. Actually, however, precisely these early statements were a tremendous success. The part of the imported science which dealt with the inspection of mental data collapsed in a surprisingly short time; even former students of Titchener were gradually converted to the new religion, and when I first came to this country a young psychologist would hesitate to confess that he was not yet entirely convinced. Whichever way he turned, all around him the Joneses in psychology were now talking Behaviorese.

What all this amounted to was, of course, that experimental psychology, which had come from Germany as a pretty narrow enterprise, became for a while narrower still in this country. The behaviorists, forever suspicious of mental facts, seemed to be afraid even of the vehicle by which such facts are in a way transmitted from one person to another, that is, of language. At any rate, many members of the new school turned away from man, who can talk, and preferred to work with animals, who cannot. But if in this fashion the scope of psychology was seriously reduced in one direction, the young science rapidly expanded in the new direction. Animal psychologists invented one technique of investigation after another, and at the present time their methods belong to the best we have. Another, and equally propitious, development soon followed. Dealing with animals as they were, some behaviorists learned to combine psychological experimentation with physiological procedures, and the result was what we now call physiological psychology. From its very beginning, physiological psychology has been mainly an American enterprise, and in other parts of the world there is little that can be compared with the work of Professor Lashley and his students. Strange things happen in the history of intellectual culture. When, in a certain period, some mistake is made by practically everybody, this very mistake has sometimes fortunate consequences.

One cannot deny, however, that the opposite also happens. The very virtues of an historical period often give birth to little affiliated vices. Who would now object to the behaviorists' admiration of science? But, unfortunately, this admiration soon went so far that concepts and techniques of natural science which are meant to be man's tools soon threatened to become the psychologists' masters. When no longer able to move along the rails laid down by the older sciences, the new scientists would feel seriously disturbed; and when asked to deal with facts, the like of which seem never to be found in physical nature, they would become both frightened and indignant. It will be my next task to illustrate these remarks by specific examples.

Some European psychologists had in the meantime recovered from that extreme devotion to experimental science which, during the early years of scientific psychology, must sometimes have been almost like a fever. One of these men, William McDougall, immigrated from Oxford just when the behaviorists were running a higher temperature than had ever been observed in Europe. Upon his arrival, and being confronted with behaviorism, he made statements more or less as follows:

The commandments of natural science must, of course, be obeyed. But the behaviorists forget to mention one such commandment, in fact, the one which should be given first rank. If in a given field we make certain observations, and particularly if we make them all the time, such observations must be accepted under all circumstances, whatever may happen elsewhere. Otherwise, why should activities in this field be honored by the name of empirical science? The behaviorists, however, not only fail to mention this commandment, they disobey it consistently. What is the reason for this strange conduct? There can be only one reason: In this fashion they are enabled to choose such facts as fit their particular philosophy, and to ignore all those which do not fit. Now there is something that clearly does not fit. Watch a rat in a maze. The most outstanding characteristic of his behavior is *striving*. Always the creature is after something, or tries to get away from something else. It is, of course, the same with man, including the behaviorist who, for a certain purpose, selects some empirical data, and refuses to recognize others. Striving is the very essence of mental life. Really, behaviorists ought to learn about the more elementary facts of life before they advertise their junior-size science.

So the immigrant from England, in spirit if not literally. It is to be regretted that, in his own later work, McDougall did not always follow the other commandments of science, those which the behaviorists rightly respected. Nothing weakened his influence upon American psychology so much as did this fact. But there is no question that he was an uncommonly courageous man. Not all scientists are willing to swim against the current which carries most of their colleagues in the opposite direction. Moreover, his main thesis, William James all over again, was undoubtedly right.

The uproar which followed McDougall's statements was

terrific. The banners of strictly scientific psychology raised high, the behaviorists counterattacked at once. Not only was McDougall obviously an armchair psychologist; far worse, he was a philosopher who had just slipped back into medieval speculation. For had not science begun its modern development when she discarded the notion that there are goals or purposes in nature? How could psychology hope to prosper if such concepts were admitted in the new science? Unperturbed, McDougall answered that, as a help in thinking and making certain observations, the armchair was probably a better instrument than many gadgets used by the experimentalists. Perhaps more armchairs and correspondingly intensified thinking were just the remedies which the behaviorists needed.

The behaviorists did not like this remark; and they indignantly rejected the suggestion that McDougall's observations, unsupported by any experimentation as they were, should be seriously considered in psychology. In the new science everything had to be just as it was in natural science, including the methods of observation and the basic characteristics of facts. It does seem that love can make people blind, even a certain love of science. In 1925, soon after my first arrival in this country, I had a curious experience. When once talking with a graduate student of psychology who was, of course, a behaviorist, I remarked that McDougall's psychology of striving seemed to me to be associated with certain philosophical theses which I found it hard to accept; but that he might nevertheless be right in insisting that, as a matter of simple observation, people do this or that in order to reach certain goals. Did not the student himself sometimes go to a post office in order to buy stamps? And did he not just now prepare himself for certain examinations to be held next Thursday? The answer was prompt: "I never do such things," said the student. There is nothing like a solid scientific conviction.

Once more we realize that the impact of European psychology upon developments in America occurred under conditions entirely different from those under which the immigration, say, of European physicists occurred in the thirties. When these physicists arrived, there was no longer any doubt what the fundamental facts, the main procedures, and the essential tasks of physics are. Irrespective of where individual physicists were born, they would therefore give any new discovery about the same place in a well-established system. Psychology, on the other hand, was almost an infant when Europeans, such as McDougall, tried to make themselves heard in America. In a science which is so young, premises of individual or national origin are bound to have a strong influence upon scientific conduct. Physicists, of course, also work with a background of convictions which is not, strictly speaking, derived from scientific evidence alone. But in physics such convictions are at least largely under the control of vast amounts of knowledge which all physicists share, and thus their convictions show great uniformity. Psychologists had no such common background at the time of McDougall's criticism. Even now, coherent bodies of knowledge develop only slowly in this young discipline, and therefore background convictions may still vary tremendously from one psychologist to another. Psychologists who love a particular form of science are, of course, also swayed by convictions which are by no means results of science. It may not have been particular scientific findings in the usual sense which made James and McDougall so strongly aware of certain phases of mental life. But surely it was not empirical evidence of any kind which caused the behaviorists' refusal to deal with these facts at all. They just knew, or believed that they knew, what can happen in the world, including its mental division; and they knew even better what cannot possibly happen in this realm. In such matters, the situation in psychology will not change until, as a consequence of the work of many, with many different backgrounds, actual knowledge forces common convictions upon all of us.

Scientific psychology is not only a creation of human beings; it also mainly deals with human beings. While, therefore, in natural science, which is supposed to study neutral facts, general convictions tend to be fairly calm, trends in psychology often depend upon convictions of a much more powerful sort. In many, these convictions refer to the very nature of man, and to what one is permitted, or not permitted, to do about him. Such people are not likely to remain entirely calm when they feel that other psychologists distort mental life into a caricature, the outlines of which are prescribed by a narrow conception of science. On the other hand, the psychologists who are so criticized will not only feel offended by this critique, which accuses them of a certain blindness, but will also be indignant when their opponents refuse to regard experimental science as the final arbiter in all matters.

In clinical psychology much use is made of so-called projective techniques. A patient is shown ink blots, or pictures of certain scenes, and is invited to interpret what he has before him. His interpretation is supposed to contain much information about his personality and his mental troubles. When we want to know what kind of people the various psychologists are, and what they believe in, we do not need such tests. Psychologists are quite eager to give us the necessary information in their articles and books—if not in so many words, at least implicitly. An understanding reader will soon know what background convictions lie behind a psychologist's work, not only because in a given instance certain topics are strongly emphasized and certain explanations consistently preferred to others, but also because some topics and possible explanations are never mentioned. Testimony of this kind is just as eloquent as any interpretations of ink blots can ever be. But why do convictions vary so much from one psychologist to another? Partly, the variations may derive from congenital differences in the make-up of individual personalities. Far more obvious, however, is the influence of the cultural climates in which the various psychologists have grown up. McDougall came to America with convictions about the nature of mental life which were inspired by the cultural tradition not only of his country but also of Europe in general. Aristotle, St. Augustine, Pascal, and Spinoza had as much to do with these convictions as had Hume and Stuart Mill. The behaviorists, too, held convictions which had arrived from Europe; but these convictions had far less illustrious sources.

At this point I should like to make a more general remark about contacts between people whose cultural traditions differ. Many take it for granted that cultural traditions constitute, without exception, subjective facts, even if the subjectivisms in question are trends of thought and feeling which history has established in whole populations. If this were right, it would, of course, be futile to argue about such traditions. As a matter of fact, well-meaning persons sometimes assure us that, if we merely made it a rule never to mention such differences among peoples as stem from the cultural histories of their various countries, the world would be a far more peaceful place. This, I believe, is dangerous advice. For how long would peace be safe if it were based on a cultural skepticism which itself is not defensible? Surely, not all effects of cultural traditions lie beyond the scope of reasonable argument. For it is also an effect of such traditions if the great importance of certain issues is clearly realized somewhere, and hardly recognized elsewhere. Suppose that, as a consequence of certain traditions, some nations have many good schools, while others have no more than a few. How can we possibly maintain that in such a case only two different national prejudices have been at work? To be sure, the various beliefs and attitudes which we find in one part of the world or another are results of historical developments. But this holds also for mathematical knowledge, a product of history which, as we all know, grew up earlier in some countries than in others. Nobody concludes that mathematics is merely an expression of national predilections. Hence, why should we assert that all other products of particular cultures are subjective in this sense? Some aspects of cultural traditions cannot, of course, be matters of serious debate, just as individuals rightly refrain from arguing about certain personal preferences. I need not give examples. But now take an Englishman who has been trained to temper political conviction with a feeling of responsibility for practical consequences. If such a man were to tell a Frenchman that traditional forms of parliamentary conduct in France might sooner or later wreck his country, would his remark express no more than a British prejudice? Again, if after studying life in the United States a Frenchman were to say that many Americans seem to work too hard for their own good, his judgment would, of course, be in line with certain traditions of his country, just as the criticized American behavior agrees with an American tradition, possibly that of Puritanism. But would it follow that the Frenchman is wrong? Most probably, national traditions represent mixtures of harmless local subjectivisms, of local shortcomings, but also of national virtues. In the cultural pattern of almost all countries there may be virtues which others have not developed to the same degree. If this is true, one country ought to be willing to be another's pupil as well as teacher.

Obviously, I am now supposing that those who, on a given occasion, happen to be teachers proceed with utmost tact, and that they always remain prepared to assume the role of pupils on the next occasion.

This applies to the contact between psychologists from Europe and their American colleagues just as it applies to more general issues. To my knowledge, no disputes between American and European psychologists have ever degenerated into antagonisms of a nationalistic kind in the usual sense of this term. But if we say this with approval, we must also repeat that not all differences of opinion in psychology which spring from different cultural traditions should, because of this origin, simply be ignored. On the contrary, some such differences are clearly proper subjects of discussion, and ways of looking at mental life which now are mainly found in a certain local tradition may very much deserve the attention of psychologists with a different tradition. The same holds, even more obviously, for local differences as to scientific procedure. As a simple example, I should like to mention that probably all European psychologists who came to this country learned from their American colleagues to be much stricter about experimental proof than they had been before. In this respect, the American tradition had been superior. But Americans were also willing to learn from those who came from Europe. The great question whether scientific psychology should be concerned with striving and purpose did not for long remain related to the difference between one kind of passport and another. Actually it was a behaviorist, Professor Tolman of California, who first admitted that purpose must be given a central position among the concepts of psychology. He also convinced other behaviorists by showing that purpose can be subjected to exact experimental investigations.

For a while, we remember, purpose had not appeared

to be acceptable in psychology because it had no counter-
part in natural science. We remarked, however, that there
was a further difficulty. As the master of young psychology,
the spirit of traditional science objected not only to certain
subject matters; it also restricted observation to particular
forms of investigation. On what evidence did McDougall
maintain that the study of purpose is a major task of psychology? He offered no results of experimentation, and no
statistics. Under the circumstances, why should a psychologist listen to him?

Although, in the present instance, this argument has
fortunately not prevailed, it is very much worth our attention, because at times it still determines a psychologist's
attitude toward new facts. The very excellence of the procedures now generally used in experimental psychology
tends to limit the scope of its investigations; for simpler
forms of observation, which are less impressive and in a
sense less precise but nevertheless altogether indispensable,
have gradually become quite unpopular. Let me say a few
words in defense of such observations.

In the first place, experimentation need not be a quan-
titative procedure. First attempts at clarification in a new
field will often be greatly facilitated if the investigator
observes in a qualitative way what happens under one
condition and another. Outstanding work of this kind has
sometimes been done even in modern physics. Secondly,
observations of the very greatest significance may also be
made without experimentation in any sense. Naturally,
psychologists from Europe are more likely to admit that
this is true than are their American colleagues, because
psychological observations of a very simple kind had been
part of the cultural tradition in Europe long before psychology learned to use experimental methods. Aristotle
knew about the association of ideas. Both he and the Arabs
were familiar with the moon illusion. Leonardo studied

the curious system formed by the various colors. Contrast, after-images, and dark-adaptation were matters of fairly general interest around 1800. When McDougall pointed to the virtual omnipresence of purpose in mental life he also simply reported what seemed to him a plain fact. As such a fact, it then became a matter of experimentation. Let us not forget that other subjects of present technical investigation in psychology have come to us from the same humble source. When Ebbinghaus invented methods by which certain forms of memory could be studied with great precision, his first questions in this field were clearly derived from a knowledge of memory which was acquired without the help of any experimentation. Everybody can gain similar knowledge in one part of psychology or another. No more is needed for this purpose than that he be interested in facts, and that he watch. Since in this fashion so much has been gained for psychology in the past, contempt for equally direct observation now and in the future would clearly be a dangerous attitude. Is further evidence to be accepted only if it is already polished with the special tools of science? I cannot believe that anybody will seriously recommend such a policy. It would deprive us of our best chances to extend our work beyond its present scope.

With these remarks in mind, we will now consider what happened when another psychological concept was imported from Europe. This concept was *insight*. It was brought over by the Gestalt psychologists. Since clouds of misunderstanding still seem to hide its meaning, I had better give a brief explanation. When a physicist wants to discover how a given system reacts to certain conditions, he observes two facts: the conditions to which the system is subjected, and the behavior of the system itself. Conditions are then varied, and if there are corresponding changes in the system, both the new conditions and the new states of the system are registered. Eventually, results are gathered in a table with two columns. In one column the various conditions which have been applied are enumerated; in the other, the corresponding states of the system are given. With considerable caution, which expresses itself in certain additional tests, it is then assumed that, when again exposed to the same conditions, the system will once more show the same reactions, and that therefore the relation between the data in the two columns represents a causal law. The physicist does not claim that causal connections as such can be observed; on the contrary, he maintains that, in his field, no such observation is possible. How, then, does the physicist protect himself against the possibility that chance rather than an actual causal connection is responsible for the relation of the data in his two columns? Since he has no means of deciding by direct observation he relies on certain indirect criteria. His whole procedure in this situation is called induction. It works to everybody's satisfaction. Curiously enough, no philosopher of science has so far been able to tell us precisely why it can be used with so much confidence.

When the first Gestalt psychologists came to this country they tried to convince their American friends that, in this respect, observation in psychology is often superior to observation in natural science. Mental facts, they said, are by no means always experienced as separate events. Rather, when we are aware of certain mental facts, we may at the same time be aware of causal relations between these facts. Actually, the immigrants maintained, instances of this kind occur in practically every moment of mental life, and among the most commonplace experiences. Suppose, for instance, that somebody lifts in succession a fountain pen and an ink pot, and that he then says, "The inkpot is heavier." Does this statement merely follow his actions as a separate further event? If we ask him, he will surely deny that this is a matter of a mere sequence in time. "When I talk," he will perhaps say, "I generally talk sense. In this particular case, for example, I knew that I talked about a relation which I had just perceived, and that the direction expressed in my statement was clearly caused by the direction found when I compared the two objects. Moreover, the latter direction, that involved in the relation as such, followed from the nature of the impressions which I had of these objects. In other words, not only were specific references of certain things to others given with these things themselves; the why of their sequence was also obvious throughout."

Another example: When a young man sees a lovely figure with a lovely face on top, and then finds himself moving in the direction of so much perfection, does he need the indirect techniques of induction for discovering that those lovely conditions and the displacement of himself as a system are causally related? Few will maintain that he does. Psychological causation may, of course, also be felt to operate in the opposite direction. Every year, before the fifteenth of March, some people make detours around their writing desks on which certain forms are spread, and find one excuse or another for being occupied elsewhere. This is called an avoidance response. In most responses of this kind those who do the avoiding know perfectly well what they avoid. Also, in our present example, the nature of the avoided objects appears to them as a most natural cause of their avoiding. Imagine somebody having to discover by induction that it is Form 1040 rather than the shape of some book on his desk which fills him with horror.

All these are instances of what the Gestalt psychologists call "insight." Some time before them, a philosopher, Wilhelm Dilthey, had the same facts in mind when he referred to *verständliche Zusammenhänge*—in English, "connections which are understood." Elementary connections in physics are not understandable for the simple reason that, as we have just seen, the physicist cannot observe such connections at all. He observes only facts of concomitance and of sequence, and can therefore never tell us what a causal connection actually is. But in psychology we have both: connections which we experience and understand, and others of which we know no more than physicists known of connections in their field. It was precisely this contrast which convinced the Gestalt psychologists that their term "insight" referred to an unmistakable characteristic of many mental situations. They did not mean, however, that insight is merely a further item which must be mentioned when so-called contents of human experience are enumerated. Rather, it was their suggestion that awareness of causal relations among mental facts largely contributes to the way in which mental activities take their course. For instance, thinking in any serious sense of the word would, from their point of view, be impossible in the absence of insight.

So far, psychologists in this country have not shown much interest in the observations to which I have just referred. And yet the very make-up of the mental world is here involved. If our awareness of a mental situation gave us only the same kind of evidence as the physicist obtains from his observations, such a situation would have to appear to us as an array of functionally unrelated facts—until the scene was studied with the techniques of induction; and the same would hold for our awareness of mental sequences. Since we actually experience that certain parts of the scene are causally related to others, any treatment of mental processes which ignores this insight is, of course, utterly misleading.

The American tradition is averse to nonexperimental forms of observation. It would therefore have been advisable not to insist too much on the simple kind of evidence from which the concept of insight had been derived. The conditions under which insight arises, and the consequences which it may have, can surely be investigated in perfectly orthodox experimentation. If a few American psychologists who did work of this kind had been more strongly supported, insight itself might gradually have been accepted by all in spite of the way in which it was first observed. Clearly it must be possible to combine the American insistence upon precise procedures with the European tendency first of all to get a good view of the phenomena which are to be investigated with so much precision. Both trends have their good points and their weaknesses. As always in the contact of two cultural traditions, optimal achievements may be expected if the weaknesses of both cancel each other, while their virtues are strengthened by coöperation.

There is no reason why we should be pessimists in psychology. We already know many things in this science, and if William James could see what we are now doing, his judgment would surely be far more favorable. He might criticize the fact that there is still less coherence among our findings than would seem desirable. But while at present this criticism would probably be justified, we need not feel discouraged on this ground. Facts in science have a way of coming together, and becoming coherent, almost on their own account. Recently I put my ear to the ground in psychology and listened. Underneath, the findings of psychology were stored just as wines are stored in French cellars. In these cellars, the wines ripen, and then taste so much better and stronger. The improvement is probably brought about by a slow chemical reaction. It seems to me that, as the result of a similar fermentation, the products of psychology are now also gaining more power. At least, while I listened, something obviously stirred in our cellar. We ought to be prepared for the time when our drink is ready. But do we all prepare ourselves?

To drop my alcoholic metaphor, occasionally a psychologist makes the impression of being somewhat tired by the debates of the past, and of not being interested in major issues for this reason. In this mood he will still do one experimental investigation after another; but he will prefer to stay within a circumscribed area in which he feels safe. It would be most unfortunate if, as a result, a certain conservatism were to develop in psychology. Actually, even outstanding men have sometimes encouraged such an attitude. For instance, it has been said with approval that psychology now tends to be eclectic. Again, we have been told that in psychology we had better stay in the middle of the road. I cannot agree with these prescriptions because, if they were followed, psychologists would have to look first of all backward. In an eclectic attitude, they would be too much concerned with ideas which are already available; and, in attempting to find the middle of the road in psychology, they would have to give too much attention to the tracks along which others have moved before them. Such attitudes could perhaps be recommended if, in research, security were an important issue. Actually there is no place for it in this field. In research, we have to look forward, and to take risks.

It is interesting to see how our great ancestors in science felt about such matters. At least in this respect, a look backward ought to be instructive. Some time ago, I therefore turned to the history of physics. The first man I saw there was Galileo. Apparently he was not at all in an eclectic mood; for he was just writing the last sentences of a devastating attack on Aristotelian physics and astronomy, his *Dialogue on the Two Chief Systems of the World, that of Ptolemy and that of Copernicus.* His face was firm and grim, and made me fear that he might actually hurl the book at the Aristotelians. My next information came to me when I was sleeping. I dreamed that I met Faraday.

"What are you now investigating?" I asked him. "Unfortunately," the great man answered, "I have no time for conversation. I am much too busy reversing figure and ground all over physics. The result will be called field physics." Clearly, Faraday had not even heard of a middle-of-the-road in natural science.

The attitudes which people assume in a science are, of course, largely determined by the situation in which this science finds itself at a given time. Some years ago, the situation in psychology may actually have been such as to make a certain amount of caution desirable. I do not believe that we need hesitate quite so much at present. In fact, the situation in psychology may soon change to such a degree that fairly long steps can be taken without fear.

The Conquest
of Theological Provincialism

Paul Tillich

When, soon after the victory of the Nazis in Germany and after my removal from the chair of philosophy at the University of Frankfort, I decided to accept an invitation to Union Theological Seminary in New York, I wrote to a friend who had already left Germany: "There is everywhere in the world sky, air, and ocean." This was my consolation in one of the most tragic moments of my life. I did not write: "I can continue everywhere my theological and philosophical work," because unconsciously I doubted whether one could do this anywhere except in Germany. This is what I mean by the term "provincialism" in the title of my paper. After having lived for a few years in the United States and having worked with theological and philosophical students and colleagues, I became aware of this formerly unconscious provincialism; and after having learned and taught several more years, the provincial outlook began to recede. And today I hope that it has disappeared, which does not mean that my German education and. the Continental European tradition which have shaped me have become ineffective. If they had, this would mean that I had fallen from one provincialism into another one, and that I had become almost useless for the American intellectual life, like some eager adoptionists amongst the refugees. But this is the other point I want to make: America can save you from European and other provincialisms, but it does not necessarily make you provincial itself. There was and there still is a give and take in this country between traditions from all over the world, which makes the growth of an American provincialism extremely difficult. This is a summary of my experience and, I believe, of that of other theological and philosophical refugees. It underlies the following theoretical analyses which will deal first with the change of our scholarly outlook after almost two decades of work in this country, and will discuss secondly the elements in our tradition which America has been more and more ready to accept.

I

If one studied theology in the first decade of this century at famous theological faculties within Germany, such as those of Tübingen, Halle, or Berlin, one identified the history of theology in the last four centuries with the history of German theology. It started with the Lutheran Reformation, it accepted or rejected elements of the thought of the Swiss Reformers, Zwingli and Calvin. It experienced the doctrinal legalism of classical orthodoxy, the enthusiastic subjectivism of the pietistic protest, the slow dissolution of the dogma of the Reformation and of the Christian dogma generally under the rational criticism of the philosophers of the Enlightenment and their theological pupils, the beginnings of historical criticism with respect to the Old and New Testaments—a movement in which the great Lessing, the classical representative of German Enlightenment, played the central role. Of course, one knew that there was an orthodox period in Western Calvinism as well as in German Lutheranism; but one considered its contribution not so much in the doctrinal as in the practical realms, in church and world politics, in personal and social ethics, things of which one always was and still is distrustful in German Lutheran theology. One also knew that there was pietism on Calvinist soil, that there was Methodism in England, and the Great Awakening in America. But one did not value very highly the theological contribution of evangelical enthusiasm and its pietistic successors. None of them was any competition for the classical tradition in theology. One also knew that the ideas of the Enlightenment originated in England and France and not in Germany. But one argued that in Catholic France they could be used only in the struggle against theology but not in support of it, and that British conformity was able to push the deistic criticisms of Bible and dogma into the background. Only in Germany, this was our feeling, was the problem of how to unite Christianity and the modern mind taken absolutely seriously.

All this was a mixture of limitation, arrogance, and some elements of truth. In the nineteenth century the belief that Protestant theology was German theology was not too far removed from the truth. The innumerable American theologians who studied in German universities in that century are witnesses to it. They usually speak more enthusiastically about the German theologians of their time than do the Germans themselves. It was the new foundation given to Protestant theology by Friedrich Schleiermacher that inaugurated this glorious period. It was the adaptation of Protestant theology to the modern mind by Ritschl and his widespread school that continued the leadership of German theology. When the greatest pupil of this school, Adolf Harnack, published his *Das Wesen des Christentums (The Nature of Christianity)* in the year 1900, it was translated into more languages than any other book except the Bible, and the Leipzig railway station was jammed by freight trains carrying Harnack's book all over the world. And when the reaction started against the theology of which Harnack's book is most representative, it was first Ernst Troeltsch in Germany and then Karl Barth in Switzerland and Germany who were the leaders. No wonder a German student of theology in the first decades of our century believed that Protestant theology is identical with German theology. It is not astonishing that he became provincial, since the province in which he lived was so large, important, and seemingly self-sustaining.

One may ask: Why did not philosophy change his attitude? The answer is simple: Because German philosophy had the same attitude. Of course it was impossible to overlook the fact that modern philosophy started in the Italy of the Renaissance, in the France of René Descartes, and the England of John Locke. One knew that the so-called philosophical century, namely the eighteenth, had its center in the France of Rousseau and Voltaire, and in the England of Berkeley and David Hume; one also realized that the great scientists of the seventeenth and eighteenth centuries were mostly French and English. But all this was overshadowed by Kant's philosophical criticism, by the rediscovery of Spinoza, by German classical philosophy as represented above all in Hegel's system, by the accompanying literature and poetry as represented above all in Goethe. It is symptomatic of the situation that we had the feeling—and here I speak autobiographically—that even Shakespeare, through the German translation by the Romanticist Wilhelm von Schlegel, had become German property. And this is not all. While, after the middle of the nineteenth century, school philosophy declined, a group of men arose who were to determine the destiny of the twentieth century: Schopenhauer, Nietzsche, and Marx, followed in the twentieth century by the fathers of modern Existentialism, the translations of the Dane Kierkegaard, the cultural criticisms of the Swiss Burkhardt, the anthropology of Jaspers, and the ontology of Heidegger. One knew about Bergson in France and William James in

America, but one considered them as exceptions. And against them stood the depth-psychological movement, the Viennese Freud, the Swiss Jung, and the other schools, most of which grew on German soil. Again the feeling arose that the philosophical movement, at least after the year 1800, was centered in Germany, as once it was centered in Greece. Where the Greeks came to an end, the Germans made a new beginning. The German philosophers are the successors of the Greek philosophers. It was especially one trait in German philosophy which, in our opinion, was the reason for its superiority: the attempt to reunite, in a great synthesis, Christianity with the modern mind. It was in its heart philosophy of religion, it was *Weltanschauung,* a vision of the world as a whole. And we despised every philosophy which was less than this.

Certainly we were aware that the literature, poetry, and drama of the period, as distinct from that of the classical period around the year 1800, had left Germany and had emigrated to the Russia of Gogol and Dostoyevsky, to the France of Flaubert and Baudelaire, to the Sweden of Strindberg and the Norway of Ibsen. But they all were available in German translations and on German stages. They became parts of the German cultural life and contributors to the German philosophical interpretation of the world.

And then it happened that, at the end of the road of German philosophy and theology, the figure of Hitler appeared. At the time of our emigration it was not so much his tyranny and brutality which shocked us, but the unimaginably low level of his cultural expressions. We suddenly realized that if Hitler can be produced by German culture, something must be wrong with this culture. This prepared our emigration to this country and our openness to the new reality it represents. Neither my friends nor I myself dared for a long time to point to what was great in the Germany of our past. If Hitler is the outcome of what we believed to be the true philosophy and the only theology, both must be false. With this rather desperate conclusion we left Germany. Our eyes were opened; but they still were dull, unable to see the reality. So we came to this country.

II

What did we see here? First, what did we see in theology? Many new things, indeed! Perhaps most important was the acquaintance with a quite different understanding of the relation between theory and practice. The independence of theory from any kind of practical application, as we were used to it in Germany, became questionable under the pragmatic-experiential approach of American theology. It was a partly disturbing, partly exciting experience when, after having read a most theoretical paper to an educated group, one was asked: What shall we do? This does not only mean: What is the practical consequence of the thing? it also means: What is the validity of the theory in the light of the pragmatic test? The background of this attitude generally, and in theology especially, is the emphasis on religious experience in the movements of evangelical radicalism which have largely formed the American mind and have made of experience a central concept in all spheres of man's intellectual life. The strong Calvinistic influence on the early periods of American history has contributed to the pragmatic approach by emphasizing the realization of the Kingdom of God in history over against the emphasis on pure doctrine in German Lutheranism. While in Continental Europe the theological faculties were the leaders of the Protestant churches, in American Protestantism the real power was in the hands of the presbytery or the corresponding bodies. Theology is not dismissed, but it is reduced to a secondary role in American Protestantism—a lesson we had to learn.

This structure of thought is not without influence on the content of theology. The glory of American theology lies neither in the historical nor in the dogmatic field, but in the sphere of social ethics. Everybody who knows something about the ecumenical movement and the structure of the World Council of Churches is aware of this fact. Whenever so-called Continental theology (meaning Continental European) clashes with Anglo-Saxon theology, it occurs in the realm of social ethics. The nature of Lutheran theology has prevented any strong development of this realm in German theological thought. Certainly the situation has changed with the rise of religious socialism and the theological support that Nazism received.

When, after the first World War, Germany was transformed by a political and social revolution of a rather radical character, the churches could not maintain their detached attitude toward politics. The King of Prussia who lost his throne was the *summus episcopus*—the supreme bishop of the Prussian Protestant church. This fall was a matter of existential concern for the church. The social groups who legally and spiritually had been the main supporters of Protestantism lost their power and were replaced by the professedly anti-religious supporters of socialism. What should be the attitude of the church to the atheistic or completely indifferent masses whose representatives came into a power to which they never had been admitted before?

Religious socialism tried to give answers to those questions, but it could influence the traditionally conservative Lutheran churches only slightly. However, they could no longer dismiss the question of the relation between the Christian message and the social revolution. Even less could they avoid the problem put before them by the Nazi conquest of Germany and the attempt of the Nazi movement to draw the churches into the orbit of their neo-pagan ideas and practices. They had no fight against state interference and persecution by Nazi organizations inside and outside the church. They could not subject themselves to state authorities who actually were the representatives of a quasi-religious faith. But even this situation produced more a detachment of the churches from the political realm than the building of a positive social ethics. Finally, the recent split of mankind into two ideological and political camps, the democratic and the communist, has forced German theologians to discuss this situation in terms of principles. But even so, hesitation and uncertainty dominate Continental theology with respect to social ethics. Karl Barth, the leading theologian in European Protestantism started as a religious socialist, turned since the period of his commentary on Paul's Epistle to the Romans in the early twenties against any kind of political theology, was forced into it again by Hitler's attack on the Protestant churches, returned to the attitude of detachment in the present East-West struggle. These oscillations are symptomatic of the difficulty in which Continental Protestantism finds itself with respect to a constructive social ethics.

As opposed to this character of Continental theology, American theological thinking is centered around social ethical problems. It surprised us to see how almost every theological problem was discussed in relation to the question of pacifism, how strong the religious color of the idea of democracy is, how the crusading spirit, in spite of all disappointments, never disappeared, how a whole period of theology was determined by the doctrines of the social gospel. The difficulties, stressed by Continental theology, in applying the absolute principles of the Christian message to concrete political situations, were met by American theological ethics in a rather ingenious way. One found that between the absolute principle of love and the ever-changing concrete situation, middle axioms exist which mediate the two. Such principles are democracy, the dignity of every man, equality before the law, etc. They are not unchangeable in the sense in which the ultimate principle is, but they mediate between it and the actual situation. This idea prevents the identification of the Christian message with a special political program. It makes it, on the other hand, possible for Christianity not to remain aloof from the actual problems of man's historical existence. In this way American theology has created a new approach to Christian social ethics, and has made the Christian message relevant not only to the relation of God and the individual person, but also to the relation of God and the world.

This attitude has presuppositions and consequences to discover which was an ever new and exciting experience. The whole history of America has turned the American mind in a horizontal direction. The conquest of a vast country with a seemingly unlimited extension, the progressive actualization of the infinite possibilities in man's dealing with nature and himself, the dynamics of Calvinism and early capitalism, the freedom from a binding tradition and from the curses of European history, all this has produced a type of thinking which is quite different from the predominantly vertical thinking in Europe. The feudal system, which gives a predetermined place to everybody, admits only rare possibilities of horizontal progress. Life is a fight in the vertical line between divine and demonic forces. It is not a struggle for the progressive actualization of human possibilities. It is hardly necessary to say that such contrasts never are absolute; but they create a predominant attitude of great theological significance. The European danger is a lack of horizontal actualization; the American danger is a lack of vertical depth. This is, for example, manifest in the way the church is used and theology is understood. In Europe the problem of the church is the problem of its ultimate foundation, and theology is supposed to explain this foundation in a completely balanced theological system. The church is above all the institution for the salvation of souls, and theology the elaboration of ultimate truth about the way of salvation. Therefore preaching and the sacraments are decisive. In American Christianity the church is a social agent, among others, which tries to surpass the others in attractiveness. Its foundations are more or less taken for granted, but the practical demands, following from its nature, are in the center of interest. Making man better, helping him to become a person, and making the social conditions better, helping them to become actualizations of the Kingdom of God on earth: this is the function of the church. Theology, in this view, has not so much the function of struggling for an adequate formulation of ultimate truth as of preparing theological students for their task as leaders of a congregation. This also must not be taken as an exclusive contrast. It is quite remarkable to see how in the last decades American theologians have tried to make theology scientifically respectable by applying experiential methods to it. It was an interesting attempt, although, I believe, not a very successful one. For what appeared in these theologies as the result of an empirical research was actually the expression of conformity to non-Christian ideas.

This leads to another surprising discovery we made in American Protestantism: its world-wide horizons. The fact of the many denominational churches shows to everybody in an existential way that there are other possibilities of Protestant expression than one's own. It points back to different lines of church-historical development since the

Reformation and before it. At the same time Protestant provincialism is avoided by the fact that, for example, the Episcopal church has, in spite of its basically Protestant theology, preserved many Catholic elements in its way of life. One of the main problems of my theology—namely, Protestant principle and Catholic substance—arose out of this experience. It implies the question: How can the radicalism of prophetic criticism which is implied in the principles of genuine Protestantism be united with the classical tradition of dogma, sacred law, sacraments, hierarchy, cult, as preserved in the Catholic churches? I had to learn that when I used the word "Catholic" in a lecture, many listeners did not think, as every Continental listener would, of the Roman Catholic church. I had to realize that there are other churches which called themselves Catholic although they had accepted most of the doctrinal tenets of Protestantism. The question is a very serious one, in view of the inner difficulties of the Protestant churches, especially the danger in which they are of becoming a moral and educational institution beside others. But I can hardly imagine that the question in this form could have been conceived within Continental Protestantism. The ecumenical point of view is further emphasized by the surprising fact that a Protestant institute such as the Union Theological Seminary is intimately connected with a Greek Orthodox institute, St. Vladimir's Theological Seminary. At the same time the opposite wing of Christian thought and life, Unitarianism, is in America a living reality and has still directly and even more indirectly a definite influence on the theological situation as a whole. The ecumenical point of view is also stressed by the fact that representatives of the so-called younger churches, those in Asia and Africa, are regular guests in the great American institutions of theological learning and ecclesiastical activity. They bring points of view into both American and Continental theology that were unknown to us within the limited horizon of German Protestantism.

Beyond all this it must be mentioned that the vivid exchange between America and the Far as well as the Near East brings, in a permanent stream, representatives of all great religions to American universities and other institutions. This makes a Christian provincialism (not to be confused with the faith in the ultimacy of the Christian message) almost impossible. An existential contact with outstanding representatives of non-Christian religions forces one into the acknowledgment that God is not far from them, that there is a universal revelation.

In spite of the variety of points of view which permanently appear within the large horizon of American theology, this is not a struggle of everyone against everyone else, but discussion, competition, and teamwork. The actual unity of Protestantism, felt by most Protestant denominations, is symbolized in an institution such as Union Theological Seminary and in the divinity schools of some great universities. It is alive in the coöperation of ministers of different denominations on the local level as well as in central organizations, such as the National Council of Churches. It is expressed in a kind of Protestant conformity which is obvious to everybody who looks at it from outside the Protestant orbit. Theologically this has led to a most radical interpenetration of denominational thinking, and beyond this it leads to the establishment of temporary or lasting organizations to which members of all the main denominations belong. This idea of theological teamwork has deep roots in American life generally and the religious life especially. It stands in marked contrast to the isolated system-builders in Continental theology—again, a lesson not easy to learn.

The last point is as valid for philosophy as for theology. The philosophical approach to reality is experiential, if

150 ·   *The Cultural Migration*

possible experimental. The validity of an idea is tested pragmatically, namely, by the function it has within the life process. This agrees with the question to which we have referred: What shall we do? The functional theory of truth is the abstract formulation of the often rather primitive way in which the question of the practical consequences of an idea is asked.

Behind the pragmatic approach to reality lies—mostly unknown to those who use it—one of the basic attitudes to reality which determined the medieval discussion, namely, nominalism. If one comes from the main tradition of Continental philosophy one soon realizes how much these traditions are dependent on what the Middle Ages called realism (which is nearer to modern idealism than to what today we call realism). In any case, it is not wrong to tell one's American students that they all are nominalists "by birth." A consequence of the nominalistic attitude is the feeling of standing at the periphery and not at the center of truth, and therefore the demand for tentative steps from the periphery towards the center, always aware of the fact that they are tentative and may lead in a wrong direction. This often produces an admirable attitude of humility, but sometimes complete rejection of a search for an ultimate truth. The positivistic, empirical attitude can be both humble acknowledgment of man's finitude and arrogant dismissal of the question of the truth which concerns us ultimately. This attitude makes understandable also the dominant role logical positivism has played in the last decades within the American philosophical scene. It can be interpreted as another expression of the humility of philosophers who want to avoid the idealistic claim that man is able to participate cognitively in the essential structure of reality. But logical positivism can also be interpreted as the desire to escape problems which are relevant to human existence. It can be interpreted as the justified distrust of an interference of emotional elements with cognitive statements. But it also can be interpreted as the dismissal of existential problems into the noncognitive sphere of feeling. The seriousness of this situation was one of the surprising discoveries we had to make when we came from traditions in which philosophy tries to build a system in which one can live. Certain words won an importance in America which they never had in Continental Europe: e.g., inquiry, investigation, research, project, etc. They all are symbolic of an attitude which is aware of one's not-having and which has the courage to ask and to seek in order to have.

Courage is another important element in American philosophical thought. Perhaps one could say that the emphasis on becoming, process, growth, progress, etc., in American philosophy is the expression of a courage which takes upon itself risks, failures, regressions, disappointments in a way which one can hardly find in the groups which are mostly responsible for Continental philosophy. They rarely resist the temptation to escape into the vertical line when the horizontal line leads to a breakdown. It was and is a moving and transforming experience to observe examples of this American "courage to be"[1] individually and nationally. One asks: What is the spiritual substance out of which this courage and its philosophical and theological expressions are born?

III

All this underlay what I have called theological and philosophical provincialism, Continental generally and German especially. The danger of the impression made upon us by these attitudes and ideas was that they would push us into another provincialism, an American one.

---

[1] Comp. my book: *The Courage to Be* (New Haven, Yale University Press, 1952).

But this is not the case. The way in which we were received when we came as refugees to the United States made it obvious that the intention on the side of our American friends was not to Americanize us, but to have us contribute in our own way to the overall American scene. Everyone was prepared for what we have to give, and nobody demanded an assimilation in which our own experiences and ideas would be subdued.

I remember discussions in which an attitude of quick assimilation was demanded by the one group while the other group maintained an attitude of tenacious resistance against adjustment to the new conditions. It was often not easy to find a way between these extremes. And it would have been impossible without the wisdom of some of our American friends who, while helping us to adapt ourselves to the new conditions, made it quite clear to us that they did not want assimilation, but original creativity on the basis of our traditions. This, it seems to me, was always so in America, and it sometimes had the effect that older European traditions were often more alive here than they were in Europe and Germany. German Ritschlianism, for instance, was still a strong force in American theology, when in Germany it had lost most of its influence. Such things, and beyond them the permanent influx of Asiatic ideas, make an American provincialism extremely unlikely.

Instead of being engulfed in American provincialism we could bring to America ideas which have influenced and will influence American thought in theology and philosophy. Without distinguishing the two, in the following survey I want to deal with some of the most conspicuous effects of the last immigration on the American intellectual life.

In the first place one must mention depth psychology—a concept which includes psychoanalysis but is much more embracing. The reasons for the astonishing victory of depth-psychological ideas in important groups of American society are manifold. One of them certainly is that they appeared in a psychotherapeutic context and not as abstract psychology, answering in this way the demand for pragmatic verification, which is so characteristic of the American mind. Related to it and strongly supported by it was the recent reception of existentialist ideas. The threat of meaninglessness was increasingly felt, especially in the younger generation of students. Existentialism does not give the answer to the question of the meaning of existence, but formulates the question in all directions and in every dimension of man's being. The Existentialism of the twentieth century is not a special philosophy or the philosophy of a few European thinkers, but it is the mirror of the situation of the Western world in the first half of the twentieth century. It describes and analyzes the anxiety of our period as the special actualization of man's basic anxiety, the anxiety which is the awareness of his finitude. Existentialism, in alliance with depth-psychology, shows the psychological and sociological mechanisms which continually give occasion to the rise of such anxiety. It reveals the amount of doubt and cynicism about human existence which permeates the Western world. It is an expression of the courage to face meaninglessness as the answer to the question of meaning. In spite of the strangeness of all this to the genuine American tradition of courage and self-affirmation it could be received, especially in its artistic, poetic, fictional, and dramatic expressions.[2] In this form its influence went beyond the educated groups, thus showing that the question of meaning is unconsciously present in many more people in the Western world than those who are able to articulate their anxiety and have the courage to take their anxiety upon themselves. It was and is possible for us who have experienced the rise of Existentialism

2 Compare my book: *The Courage to Be.*

in Europe to interpret its meaning to our American listeners in a genuine existential way.

One may ask whether there is an "Existentialist" theology. Certainly in Kierkegaard we have both one of the profoundest and most original analyses of man's situation in anxiety and despair and, at the same time, a theological answer which lies in the tradition of Lutherian pietism. In the theological school of Karl Barth, which often is called neo-orthodox, we find the same two elements, Existentialist questions and traditional answers, not pietistic, but orthodox. More adequately than the theology of these men, that of Rudolf Bultmann could be called Existentialist. Bultmann is dependent on both Kierkegaard and Barth, but beyond both of them he is a great New Testament scholar, maintaining the tradition of higher criticism in a most radical and uncompromising way. He uses the Existentialist analyses of the human situation as the key for the understanding of the mythological elements in the New Testament. Existential analysis deciphering the riddles of the biblical myth: This is what one could call Existentialist theology.

American theology as a whole has strongly resisted the influx of neo-orthodoxy in its genuine form. But it has received many special ideas and emphases, especially if they appeared in a less supranaturalistic and authoritarian form than that developed by Barth, as for instance in Bultmann.

This refers, for instance, to the interpretation of history. Again, there are many causes for the decline of the progressivistic interpretation of history in American thought. There are the continual disappointments about the course of history from the end of the First World War up to the present events, day by day. But there is also the impact of the new understanding of human nature as it was introduced into America by the alliance of theological analysis, psychology, and Existentialist literature and art. In the fight against the utopia of progress the Europeans who had come to this country joined and strengthened the anti-utopian forces which were latently present in genuine American groups and personalities (as, for example, Reinhold Niebuhr).

Historical consciousness generally was something we brought from historically minded Europe to unhistorically minded America. It is not a matter of historical knowledge, but a matter of a feeling which every European instinctively has, namely, that ideas are in their very nature historical. The development of an idea is an essential element in the idea itself. This is the background of what was called *Geistesgeschichte* (inadequately translated "intellectual history" or "history of thought"). The true meaning of *Geistesgeschichte* is not a factual history of former thoughts, but is the attempt to make visible the implications and consequences of an idea in the light of its history. In this sense *Geistesgeschichte* is a part of systematic philosophy and theology. The assertion is rather unfamiliar to most American students, and it was one of our most important tasks to balance the American emphasis on new beginning with the European emphasis on tradition. And it was equally important to balance the American emphasis on facts with the European emphasis on interpretation.

The question we ask ourselves after almost two decades of participation in the American spiritual life is: Will America remain what it has been to us, a country in which people from every country can overcome their spiritual provincialism? One can be both a world power politically and a provincial people spiritually. Will the present emphasis on the "American way of life" produce such a situation? There is a serious danger that it will. The

America to which we came was wide open. It liberated us without restricting us to new spiritual limitations. For this America we shall fight against any groups working for American provincialism and for an America in which every provincialism, including theological and philosophical provincialism, is resisted and conquered.

The Academic Profession

An Arno Press Collection

Annan, Noel Gilroy. **Leslie Stephen: His Thought and Character in Relation to His Time.** 1952

Armytage, W. H. G. **Civic Universities: Aspects of a British Tradition.** 1955

Berdahl, Robert O. **British Universities and the State.** 1959

Bleuel, Hans Peter. **Deutschlands Bekenner** (German Men of Knowledge). 1968

Bowman, Claude Charleton. **The College Professor in America.** 1938

Busch, Alexander. **Die Geschichte des Privatdozenten** (History of Privat-Docentens). 1959

Caplow, Theodore and Reece J. McGee. **The Academic Marketplace.** 1958

Carnegie Foundation for the Advancement of Teaching. **The Financial Status of the Professor in America and in Germany.** 1908

Cattell, J. McKeen. **University Control.** 1913

Cheyney, Edward Potts. **History of the University of Pennsylvania: 1740-1940.** 1940

Elliott, Orrin Leslie. **Stanford University: The First Twenty-Five Years.** 1937

Ely, Richard T. **Ground Under Our Feet:** An Autobiography. 1938

Flach, Johannes. **Der Deutsche Professor der Gegenwart** (The German Professor Today). 1886

Hall, G. Stanley. **Life and Confessions of a Psychologist.** 1924

Hardy, G[odfrey] H[arold]. **Bertrand Russell & Trinity:** A College Controversy of the Last War. 1942

Kluge, Alexander. **Die Universitäts-Selbstverwaltung** (University Self-Government). 1958

Kotschnig, Walter M. **Unemployment in the Learned Professions.** 1937

Lazarsfeld, Paul F. and Wagner Thielens, Jr. **The Academic Mind:** Social Scientists in a Time of Crisis. 1958

McLaughlin, Mary Martin. **Intellectual Freedom and Its Limitations in the University of Paris in the Thirteenth and Fourteenth Centuries.** 1977

Metzger, Walter P., editor. **The American Concept of Academic Freedom in Formation:** A Collection of Essays and Reports. 1977

Metzger, Walter P., editor. **The Constitutional Status of Academic Freedom.** 1977

Metzger, Walter P., editor. **The Constitutional Status of Academic Tenure.** 1977

Metzger, Walter P., editor. **Professors on Guard:** The First AAUP Investigations. 1977

Metzger, Walter P., editor. **Reader on the Sociology of the Academic Profession.** 1977

Mims, Edwin. **History of Vanderbilt University.** 1946

Neumann, Franz L., et al. **The Cultural Migration:** The European Scholar in America. 1953

Nitsch, Wolfgang, et al. **Hochschule in der Demokratie** (The University in a Democracy). 1965

Pattison, Mark. **Suggestions on Academical Organization with Especial Reference to Oxford.** 1868

Pollard, Lucille Addison. **Women on College and University Faculties:** A Historical Survey and a Study of Their Present Academic Status. 1977

Proctor, Mortimer R. **The English University Novel.** 1957

Quincy, Josiah. **The History of Harvard University.** Two vols. 1840

Ross, Edward Alsworth. **Seventy Years of It:** An Autobiography. 1936

Rudy, S. Willis. **The College of the City of New York:** A History, 1847-1947. 1949

Slosson, Edwin E. **Great American Universities.** 1910

Smith, Goldwin. **A Plea for the Abolition of Tests in the University of Oxford.** 1864

Willey, Malcolm W. **Depression, Recovery and Higher Education:** A Report by Committee Y of the American Association of University Professors. 1937

Winstanley, D. A. **Early Victorian Cambridge.** 1940

Winstanley, D. A. **Later Victorian Cambridge.** 1947

Winstanley, D. A. **Unreformed Cambridge.** 1935

Yeomans, Henry Aaron. **Abbott Lawrence Lowell: 1856-1943.** 1948